Why Lyrics Last

Why Lyrics Last

EVOLUTION, COGNITION,
AND SHAKESPEARE'S SONNETS

Brian Boyd

HARVARD UNIVERSITY PRESS
Cambridge, Massachusetts
London, England
2012

Library of Congress Cataloging-in-Publication Data

Boyd, Brian, 1952–
Why lyrics last : evolution, cognition, and Shakespeare's sonnets / Brian Boyd.
p. cm.
Includes bibliographical references and index.
ISBN 978-0-674-06564-2 (alk. paper)
1. Shakespeare, William, 1564–1616. Sonnets.   2. Sonnets, English—History
and criticism.   3. Lyric poetry—History and criticism.   I. Title.
PR2848.B68   2012
821'.3—dc23   2011040339

To Bronwen

and to Mac Jackson, *Sonnets* sleuth supreme

Contents

SHAKE-SPEARES SONNETS, 1609

    Envoi: Verse and Aversion   175

    Notes   185

    Bibliography   199

    Index   215

Acknowledgments

I have written several of my books, after much research and reflection, in a rapid chain reaction of recognitions. Since *Why Lyrics Last* followed this rhythm, I do not have the usual long academic list of readers to thank. I owe particular thanks to Mo Cohen of Gingko Press for inviting me to work on Nabokov's poem "Pale Fire" (after looking at it closely, I could see no adequate comparison to its verbal effects but Shakespeare's sonnets); to Joseph Carroll, in his role as editor of *Evolutionary Review,* for encouraging me to write an essay on verse; and especially to MacDonald P. Jackson. In the absence of external evidence, the painstaking, meticulous, and far-reaching empirical and critical work he has done on Shakespeare's sonnets since the early 1960s at last provides a basis for understanding something of the poems' compositional chronology. Mac, John Kerrigan, Jonathan Gottschall, Robin Headlam Wells, Marcus Nordlund, and Paul Seabright all read the manuscript with judicious care; I am especially grateful for the detailed and thoughtful suggestions from Jon and Marcus. Sam Bookman performed invaluable bibliographic work as my research assistant. My editor at Harvard, John Kulka, has as always been a pleasure to work with and, as usual, economically astute with suggestions. Once again Ann Hawthorne has been a vigilant but gentle editor. And, as always, Bronwen Nicholson has been my unfailing encourager and eager first reader.

For permission to incorporate material from "Verse: Universal? Adaptive? Aversive?" (2011), thanks to the editors of *Evolutionary Review;* from "Why We Love Fiction" (2010), to the editors of *Axess;* and from *"Pale Fire: A Poem in Four Cantos" by John Shade* (2011), to Gingko Press. The Emily Dickinson poem in Chapter 2 is reprinted by permission of the publishers and the Trustees of Amherst College from *The Poems of Emily Dickinson: Reading Edition,* edited by Ralph W. Franklin, Cambridge, Mass.: The Belknap Press of Harvard University Press, copyright © 1998, 1999 by the President and Fellows of Harvard College, copyright © 1951, 1955, 1979, 1983 by the President and Fellows of Harvard College. For permission to reproduce her poem "Anne Hathaway," thanks to Carol Ann Duffy.

Why Lyrics Last

Introduction

Story and Verse

When did you last immerse yourself in a pool of make-believe? In a television drama, or a film, watched from the sofa or a cinema seat? A story you read to your children last night, or the novel you settled down with later? The comic strip in this morning's newspaper? A joke you heard at work or around the table? Chances are that the last fictional story you encountered was not long ago, and the previous one not long before that.

When did you last encounter verse? Again, probably not long ago, in song or hymn lyrics or in advertising jingles. Had you lived in Homer's day, or in Virgil's, Dante's, or Chaucer's, or even in Shakespeare's or Byron's, you might have met story and verse together; but more recent ways of telling stories on page and screen make you unlikely to reach for verse when you crave a story.[1] And when did most of us who are not poets or literature teachers or students last read a serious poem, or a book of poems?

"Poetry" has no rhyme in English. Even for many literature students, the first near-rhyme for "poetry" to leap to mind might well be "lavatory," somewhere they'd rather not linger. They just don't "get" poetry, they confess: verse, what could be worse? Yet even those who profess not to understand poetry enjoy rhymes in rock songs, punchy rhythms in rap, playful alliterations and puns in advertising and headlines. They and others enjoyed nursery rhymes, schoolyard chants and rhyming games when they were children, and will pass some of them on to *their* children.

Like others, I feel confident we can learn more about literature and life by discovering more about the why and how of our minds. How might evolution—the why—and cognition—the how—explain why we love the ingredients of poetry but why so many find the whole dish of literary poetry a little heavy, oversauced, hard to digest? And why despite that do *some* poems invite end-less resavoring?[2]

Literature in the broadest sense, from nursery rhymes to *King Lear* and from *Gilgamesh* to hypertext fiction and video games, has two main strands, narrative and verse. They often intertwine, sometimes tightly, in the *Iliad, Paradise Lost,* or *Eugene Onegin,* sometimes loosely, in *Hamlet* (part verse, part prose), or almost not at all, as I will argue is the case in Shakespeare's sonnets (all verse, but without the defined sequences of concrete events that distinguish narrative). In my previous book in this vein, *On the Origin of Stories: Evolution, Cognition, and Fiction,* I sought to explain why a species like ours, which thrives through its superior handling of information, should find the untrue information of fiction so irresistibly engrossing. Now in this sequel I focus on verse, especially verse in its purest form, lyric, verse without story—partly because both we evolutionary literary critics and *our* critics

have been aware that literary evolutionism has focused overwhelmingly on narrative and little on verse (as one review of three books
on epic poetry ends: "it remains unclear what, if anything, evolutionary literary criticism has to say about poetry itself").[3] Now
I wish to ask: Why, unlike narrative, does verse by itself seem so
much less compelling to many, yet why do some lyrics last so
triumphantly?

In *On the Origin of Stories* I stressed the centrality of narrative
to human thought and literary art. Narrative seems highly likely
to be the default task orientation of the human mind. By that I
mean that if our minds can process information in narrative terms,
they automatically will. Narrative allows us to understand where
we have come from and where we are so that we can predict or
plan where we might soon move. It therefore shapes much of our
thought and much of our literature.

But not all. It may be powerful, but not all-powerful. We can
see or assay other kinds of patterns than those of character and
intention, cause and effect: propositions ("From fairest creatures
we desire increase"), arguments ("dear my love, you know, / You
had a father, let your son say so"), analogies ("Like as the waves
make towards the pebbled shore, / So do our minutes hasten to
their end"), emotions ("For thy sweet love remembered such wealth
brings / That then I scorn to change my state with kings"), and
patterns in words rather than their referents, in sound and syntax
as well as sense ("since first your eye I eyed"). Because narrative
shapes so much of our thought, because it offers such a powerful
way of understanding our world, it engages and holds our attention. But because *all* kinds of pattern appeal to our appetite
for ordered information, we often also encounter other patterns
brought in to support those of narrative, like the patterns of the
verse line that structure oral or written epic, or the musical ac-
companiment for stories from Homer to Hollywood.

In narrative, patterns converge on unfolding situations. But sometimes the sheer appeal of other kinds of patterns, not necessarily convergent, also shapes literature. That passion for nonnarrative pattern reaches its most concentrated form in lyrics—in poems without stories.

I wanted to call this book *On the Absence of Stories,* but my publishers thought the title alarmingly negative. I meant to imply something much more positive: to identify the pleasures that verse can offer *aside* from those of narrative.

I like classics, works that last over time and place and repeated rereadings and successive life-stages. In *On the Origin of Stories* I chose as my two examples Homer's *Odyssey,* as a classic from early in our collective history of story, and Dr. Seuss's *Horton Hears a Who!,* as a classic from early in our individual enjoyment of story. For a sequel that would take us from Shakespeare to Spiegelman, I also wanted to include verse as well as narrative, and planned to begin with Shakespeare's sonnets before moving on to *Hamlet* and *Twelfth Night,* only to find the sonnets demanding a book by themselves.

Shakespeare's sonnets are the prototypical lyrics in English, and perhaps the most successful in Western literature, but for all their fame, they are rarely read *in toto. Shake-speares Sonnets,* as the first edition of 1609 was called, sells more in modern editions than any other single Shakespeare work, yet it remains the most problematic of lyric collections, provoking more published criticism than any other work in the Shakespeare canon except the notoriously enigmatic *Hamlet.* The sonnets raise in their sharpest form questions about the relationships between lyric and narrative, between the brevity of lyrics and the scope of lyric sequences, and between individual lyrics and their contexts.

As I tackled the sonnets, I discovered grounds for concluding that after having made his mark in dramatic and narrative verse, Shakespeare sought in the sonnets to stake a third perch on Parnassus by testing what he could do as a writer *without* stories. This is not at all how some read the sequence: poet Don Paterson, in his exuberantly irreverent recent reading, declares that "The Sonnets have to be read as a narrative of the progress of love."[4] I will argue that, on the contrary, Shakespeare sought to construct his collection in the absence of stories, and that this aim is precisely what has made the volume both the most successful and the most tantalizing and unresolvable of lyric sequences. The *Sonnets* therefore offer a perfect opportunity to focus on the appeal of verse apart from the attractions of embedded narrative.

In *On the Origin of Stories* I characterized all art as cognitive play with pattern, and explored our innate attraction to information that we can see as patterned, since if we recognize patterns we can process information rapidly, in real time. I then discussed art, especially the art of fiction, in terms of the appeal artists make for the attention of audiences through their handling of patterns upon patterns.

In *Why Lyrics Last* I examine the appeal of the patterns that combine in lyric verse; the resistance to the demands often made by this hyperconcentration of pattern in pure lyric, especially if it lacks the effortless ordering and emotional engagement that story provides; and the way lyrics that last blend the appeal of pattern with other strategies for attention.

I argue that Shakespeare, having already achieved fame in drama and narrative verse, sought in his sonnets to explore the possibilities of verse without stories, through patterns and relationships unrestricted by the shapes stories impose. As a major storyteller, he knows how to harness the emotional intensity that makes drama and narrative so alluring. As a poet, he capitalizes on the apparent immediacy of access to the poet's mind that lyrics allow both addressee and audience. That combination makes the most famous of his sonnets among the most engaging and enduring ever written.

But in fact Shakespeare omits and obstructs any story, even where he seems to imply it. He beguiles but he blocks, and no wonder readers for centuries have searched for a narrative but never found it. He never forfeits the energies to be gained by appealing to our default inclination to construe information in narrative terms if we possibly can, but in the free space that the absence of stories allows, he multiplies patterns within sonnets, between sonnets, and within the whole sequence, inviting us back again and again to discover new patterns and new pleasures from endless new perspectives.

Lyrics Unlinked

I

Poetry, Pattern, and Attention

Art as Adaptation

In *On the Origin of Stories* I proposed an explanation of art in general and the art of fiction in particular. Art, I suggested, derives from play, widespread in many animal species and perhaps universal in mammals. Play offers animals with flexible behavior—behavior that cannot be completely specified genetically and can be modified by learning—the chance to develop and refine expertise. Practice in key behaviors in safe conditions offers such advantages that it evolved to become irresistibly self-motivating, to become *fun*.

Since flight and fight can make the most urgent difference to survival, play running, chasing and fighting are by far the commonest animal play behaviors. For humans, however, survival depends to a unique extent not just on physical but especially on mental advantages, on our ability to acquire and manipulate information.

Like other animals, we can process the huge amount of potential information in the world swiftly, in real time, only when it forms patterns that our minds can recognize. "The brain evolved to predict, and it does so by identifying patterns."[1] Detecting patterns within information enables minds—or even organisms without minds—to "understand" or respond to their environment efficiently. We may notice the pattern of lengthening or shortening days, but not as accurately as many plants can.

On the other hand, as animals, and extremely social animals at that, we are highly attuned to tracking information patterns that indicate the actions, intentions, dispositions, and characters of members of our own species or others. Our minds naturally take in sensory information about lines, colors, and sounds and send it up to mental convergence zones for further processing in terms of objects, agents, and movements.[2] They then take that higher-level output as input for still further processing at super-convergence zones, in terms of patterns of action and intention, character, role and situation, causes and consequences. We cannot help thinking in terms of narrative pattern.

And as animals so socially disposed as to have evolved language, we are particularly attuned to the patterns of sound and sense in the languages we know. When recording devices track acoustic frequencies to analyze speech sounds objectively, they show continuous variation between distinct but related phonemes (*b* and *p*, for instance) and continuous sound production across what we hear as syllable and word breaks. Even as infants we filter out the informational noise that tape recorders cannot help registering and begin to extract the patterns of phonemic distinctions in the language of our birth environment.[3]

We humans have an appetite for *open-ended* pattern, not only the patterns we evolved to detect automatically. Vervet monkeys signal to one another in different ways when they see snakes, or leopards, or eagles, because they need to react in different ways to different threats, but they never learn to associate fresh snake or leopard tracks with the likelihood of either in the vicinity. Human trackers in the Kalahari or the Australian desert, on the other hand, over time master the local patterns that enable them to track prey and kin, and medical researchers now tease out the causal patterns linking particular chemicals to particular cancers.

To encompass art in all its diversity, from infant to adult, from lullabies to Lully or Lady Gaga, I characterize its common core as *cognitive play with open-ended pattern.*[4] Just as animal physical play refines performance, flexibility, and efficiency in key behaviors, so human art refines our performance in our key perceptual and cognitive modes, in sight (the visual arts), sound (music), and social cognition (story). These three modes of art, I propose, are adaptations. Like others, that is, I claim that they show evidence of special design in humans, design that offers survival and especially reproductive advantages.[5]

Our motivation to engage in these modes of art from the nursery to the rest home ensures that we refine our ability to produce and process patterns in our most powerful information systems. We incrementally fine-tune our neural wiring through our repeated and focused engagement in each of the arts. Fiction in particular, by harnessing the advanced power of human social cognition, our ability and inclination to track the actions, intentions, and thoughts of others, also expands our imaginations so that we can make sustained forays into possibility space.

Might verse, too, be adaptive?

Verse: Universal? Adaptive? Aversive?

If vision and hearing are our richest senses, and social cognition our most complex form of evolved thought, language offers us our most powerful and precise form of communication, even with ourselves. It would be surprising if our disposition to play with pattern did not also manifest itself in language. And indeed we have a strong motivation to play in this domain. Infants babble at a few months. A few months later, adults engage them in the rhythmic, multimedia turn-taking which developmental psychologists call protoconversation, and which has rightly been seen as a precursor of art and especially poetry.[6] Children progress to nursery rhymes ("Hickory dickory dock"), rhyming games ("Ring-a-ring o' roses"), challenges ("A pinch and a punch for the first of the month"), and taunts ("Tell-tale tit, your tongue will split, And all the little puppy-dogs will have a little bit"). They pass through a stage of enjoying the puny puns in candy wrappers and Christmas crackers. The developmental evidence shows that play with verbal pattern begins early and suggests that it forms an essential part of our acquisition of rich verbal skills.[7]

Verbal play does not stop in childhood. From adolescence we develop a special interest in love songs. For adults, play with language patterns not only pervades the verbal arts, drama, verse, song, fiction, and comedy from sitcom to standup, but regularly hooks attention in advertising, brand names, book titles, graffiti, and headline-writing; in the persuasive arts of political and other debate; and, in sheer humor, to relax social tension and enhance social lubrication.

Language Play before Verse

We have a high sensitivity to pattern in language and a high inclination to play with language. But although the sensitivity and the inclination are central to verse, they are not unique there. Play with verbal pattern can be artful wherever we find it, in the most successful of brand names, Coca-Cola, or the dandruff shampoo Head and Shoulders (head and shoulders above other products that also try to keep dandruff off your head and shoulders), or the headlines that catch our eye and perhaps haunt our memories by reworking familiar phrases. I will never forget, much as I'd like to, the *Times Literary Supplement* header for a review of a book about prostitution: "Slut Machines."

Patterns beyond the norm, patterns that violate expectations, compel us from childhood and extend our verbal reach, from babbling to nursery rhymes and beyond. They also attract our attention as adults. The many manifestations of patterned play in language across time, place, and life-stage suggest that we have an evolved human predisposition for play with the patterns of language.

Nevertheless I suggest that our language play probably does *not* constitute an adaptation of its own. It derives from the common animal predilection for pattern and the even more marked and more widespread animal predisposition to play, and from the human fusion of these that has led to what I have proposed as the key adaptation behind art, our unique human motivation to play with pattern. Our predisposition to play with the patterns of language helps fine-tune minds in language acquisition and use. That seems likely to be a by-product of already evolved features, since the motivation to play with pattern appears to have established itself in visual art and music, and quite probably in mime, several hundred thousand years ago, before modern human language.[8]

The ability to play with the patterns of language may have needed no extra cognitive design—the necessary condition for this inclination to qualify as an adaptation. But given that the capacity to handle language well would have been strongly selected for, there may have been additional tweaking of motivational systems to produce an especially strong or an especially focused predisposition to play with words. Whether this occurred or not, and whether our play with language therefore involves an additional adaptation or remains simply a by-product that plugs language into an existing predisposition for play with pattern, are questions that need to be tested empirically, if we can find ways to do so.

Apart from the obvious individual developmental advantages of mastering language, our inclination to play with verbal pattern may also have yielded social advantages even before the advent of verse. Proverbs, ubiquitous across cultures, constitute a kind of proto-poetry. Refined collectively as well as individually, they become attention-catching, efficiently compact, and memorable through play with pattern in multiple modes. Take "A stitch in time saves nine." Only a third the length of a haiku, this proverb has many of the hallmarks of verse: sound patterns, alliteration (*s*titch-*s*aves) and assonance (t*i*me-n*i*ne); rhythmic pattern, in the iambic (tee TUM) stress of "a STITCH in TIME saves NINE," with a partial stress on *saves* interestingly modulating the regularity; the concrete imaginative prompt of "stitch," and its surprise conjunction with the abstract "time"; the defamiliarizing, slightly misleading "stitch in" (as if it might continue "stitch in cloth," say, or "stitch in that hem"), which, I suspect, was what made me ask my mother to explain the proverb when I first heard it; the economy, in the ellipsis of "nine" (rather than "nine stitches," or "nine more"), which itself exemplifies the economy of time the proverb recommends.

Proverbs reflect not only internal patterns of language but also patterns in life useful in shaping decision and action: here, that attending swiftly to a problem may spare much more effort in future. Proverbs supply behavioral rules of thumb in compact and memorable forms—forms that can therefore be easily recalled and quickly dispensed on the fly because their concreteness activates and resonates in our imaginations.

Children's verbal play, like much of their pretend story play, tends to be fanciful and nonsensical. Within the security of adult supervision and the safety of human settlement, children can explore widely and freely. Adults by contrast must confront the real world. Especially in ancestral environments and oral cultures, though also even in modern print- and screen-saturated worlds, proverbs have provided an arresting, efficient way of preserving, compacting, and relaying knowledge. In cultures like that of the Kuranko of Sierra Leone, the ability to quote the appropriate proverb at the right moment is prized as a sign of wisdom,[9] and surely this was so elsewhere before formal schooling became the norm. Unlike poetry in modern cultures, which prize innovation and individuality, and unlike the messages passed on in the game of "telephone" or Chinese whispers, which disintegrate comically in the course of repeated transmission, proverbs have been handed on and honed collectively to maximize their accuracy, memorability, and transmissibility. Societies have presumably benefited from having their values encapsulated and shared in rapidly, reliably reproducible form, while individuals have earned esteem for their store of apt apothegms.

Verse

Proverbs take to a high pitch the play with patterns in language and life that we also find in verse, and their efficiency in passing on shared values may well have offered adaptive advantages. But verse is more specific than play with verbal pattern. Although verse exists across cultures,[10] it seems less an adaptation in itself than a specific cultural device—a "Good Trick," in Daniel Dennett's term,[11] a trick good enough to have found its way to cultures around the world, or perhaps to have been repeatedly discovered independently. All verse depends on line length, on lines that usually take two to three seconds to utter—according to one explanation, the length of the human auditory present, our capacity to hold a sequence of sounds in our head at once;[12] according to another, the size of working memory, which can cope with five to seven different chunks of information.[13]

The only common feature of verse across languages is that in verse, poets determine where lines end—in accordance with their sense of what audiences can take in at a given moment. In casual conversation, by contrast, utterance lengths are shaped unpredictably by content, turn-taking conventions, the assurance and enthusiasm of speakers, and their sensitivity to auditors' reactions. In prose (not the same as conversational speech, *pace* Molière's Monsieur Jourdain), line length is entirely incidental, determined only by the relative size of handwritten, printed, or pixilated characters, on the one hand, and pages or screens, columns, and margins on the other. We can reset poems as prose by removing the line-ends that the poets have determined. We could take a newspaper or encyclopedia article, or even an essay by a great prose stylist, and arrange it as poetry, but it would be flat poetry. But if exactly the same words in the same order can be set as prose or poetry, what makes the difference?

Poets control our attention by making us focus on particular groups of words in one mental moment: as Cleanth Brooks and Robert Penn Warren note, the line is a "unit of attention."[14] Prose writers tend to focus primarily on their subject matter, and will shape our attention only insofar as the content requires. But poets arrange lines (or the speech units rendered as written lines) so that each comes under the undivided spotlight of our attention before we move to the next. Or, to switch from a visual metaphor to a more appropriate auditory one, since poetry began long before the invention of writing: poetry holds the mind's ear, in lines that take around three seconds to say. Poets of course have not known that they were constructing lines to fit the human auditory present, or the capacity of working memory; but that's what they have discovered, by trial and error, because that length holds human attention better, more concentratedly, than longer or bitsier units.

Verse, in other words, employs language to fit a humanly universal cognitive constraint. Controlling one's attention matters for any conscious creature facing a world teeming with potential information, but in humans attention attains a unique importance. Unlike other species, we value joint attention: from the age of nine or ten months, we check back and forth to see that others are attending to what we want them to attend to.[15] Sharing attention reaches an unprecedented level in humans even before we acquire language; it makes language possible; and language in turn allows the sharing of attention to things absent and even remote and unforeseen, hypothetical, counterfactual, or impossible.[16]

Evolutionary and cognitive considerations strengthen our reasons for foregrounding attention as a prime concern in any art: our synaptic pathways can be transformed over time by small incremental steps, provided our attention engages fully in the activity.[17] Artists and advertisers, as well as rare academicians from Aristotle on, have recognized the centrality of attention for art, but most academic critics, paid to attend to works of art or to direct their students' attention that way, have all too often taken attention for granted and focused on abstractable, discussable meanings. Reconsidering art in terms of attention can revalorize popular art and invite a richer analysis of artistic strategy even in high art, and a clearer evaluation of the audience costs and benefits of the attention particular works solicit.

By its very nature, poetry makes a unique appeal to attention. In fitting the cognitive constraint of working memory, it allows us to release information in verbal bursts that reliably, repeatedly direct the attention of an audience to fix exactly on a specified segment of sense. No wonder this offers such an advantage that it has become a cultural universal, and no wonder poetry seems to many the essence of all art.

When poets focus audience attention on lines whose lengths they control—through pause and intonation in speech, or through lineation in print—they can invite closer scrutiny of each line. The slight lingering and the slight increase in emphasis at the end of the line, in the delivery of an accomplished speaker of verse,[18] or the blank on the page at the end of a line in written verse, can offer a space for assimilation, appreciation, reflection, and resonance. Verse therefore tends to make the most of the line as a unit of attention, by heightening the play with verbal pattern that I have proposed we are adapted for, and the play with thought that human cognitive flexibility independently allows.[19]

Patterns such as rhythm, rhyme, and syntactic or sonic parallelism, independently or together, serve to demarcate and integrate lines of verse in different traditions: rhythm in Homeric hexameter or English blank verse, rhyme in many European traditions, syntactic parallelism in Hebrew verse, alliteration in old Germanic verse. Because the initial and final sounds of words have particular cognitive salience, alliteration and rhyme are particularly prominent in traditional verse forms. Devices like rhyme not only accentuate line endings but also set up patterns between lines, particularly satisfying because the repeated rhyme sound echoes a previous sound already just out of working memory but available for swift recall and reinspection. (Repetition plays an even more prominent role in music and dance, the other most time-focused arts, and hence also in song, fusing as it does verse and music.) And because verse lines offer a controlled dose of information, poets writing and audiences reading tend to seek innovative images to invent or imbibe during the slight pause that the line-ends allow.

As we have seen, proverbs offer mnemonic advantages, especially in preliterary cultures, through their concentration of patterns. So, too, does verse. Verse makes it possible to control the rhythm of information release in longer texts, while the patterns repeated from line to line offer a scaffold of structure on which memory can reconstruct, and therefore serve to recall and stabilize texts.[20] The concentrated patterns of rhythm and rhyme can aid in the transmission of longer texts, especially those of myths, legends, and religious or other lore or ritual felt to be important enough to be passed on more or less exactly. The work of the Homerist Milman Parry and those he inspired shows prodigious feats of memory accomplished by the bards of Yugoslavia and elsewhere (Africa, central Asia) who recited oral epics.[21] The mnemonic advantages of the transmission of socially shared information may well have been adaptive for group selection, bolstering social cohesion through the reliable rehearsing of narratives incorporating and communicating shared knowledge and values.[22]

Similar principles operate in ritual chant or song (psalms, hymns, the songs of African praise-singers). The rhythmic patterns of verse can allow for emotional attunement and physical entrainment. Emotional attunement matters for any social species, and especially for ultrasocial humans,[23] and operates constantly through the changing contours of narrative, amplified for many ancient bards and modern filmgoers by accompanying music. Verse rarely lacks any narrative elements, even if does not tell whole stories, and some, like the renowned Maori warrior chief Te Rauparaha's battle song *Ka mate ka ora,* takes emotional attunement to levels of fierce intensity. Mere physiological entrainment, attunement to rhythms, links us to one another and imparts a confidence in ourselves even at the individual level. Just as we walk more smoothly in a steady rhythm, and perform group actions far better with a steady *shared* rhythm (hence work songs for sailors, Volga boatmen, chain gangs, and Dinka potmakers), so we feel enhanced pleasure and control from the perception, even if unconscious, of regular rhythm. In most cultures we express and enjoy physical entrainment to the rhythms of music in the form of dance or clapping and tapping. We also notice with a new jab of surprised attention a variation on the expected rhythm.

Even orally composed lines like Homer's were regulated by pattern—in his case especially by the rhythm of dactylic hexameter. But when poets learned to write, they had much more opportunity to maximize the play with pattern in each line and the pause for assimilation afterward.[24] Once the slight pauses in time and the slight shifts in intonation that demarcated spoken lines were rendered as gaps, as line breaks in space; once they appealed also to our dominant sense, sight; and once writers and readers could linger over them as they chose, lines could become even more the "units of attention" that Brooks and Warren define them as. The space around a poem's lines, and perhaps even around its entirety, if it is too short to sketch a story, may invite readers to linger,[25] whether for the cognitive challenge of a riddle, from Babylonian verse to Dickinsonian, or for the lingering emotional reverberations of poems like haiku. Poets recognize the competition for audience attention, and they cannot track readers' responses as they can those of live audiences. They need to compensate to be sure of engaging their absent audiences by multiplying the appeals to attention, especially should they wish to forgo the emotional engagement that narrative almost automatically supplies. They therefore appeal to readers especially by the play of patterns at the levels of sound, word, and phrase; of thought, in images, metaphors, generalizations, and arguments; and of line-units, stanzas, and other higher-level forms.

Competition for readers encourages poets to maximize the attention-earning power of the line. Researchers in the empirically focused Daniel Berlyne–Colin Martindale tradition of the psychology of art stress the competition for attention through novelty.[26] Their claims have been boosted by the recent emphasis in neuroscience on the importance of prediction errors in mental processing. Minds predict features of their environments, which normally do not change rapidly from moment to moment. They tend to notice only what escapes their prediction, and they actually receive a dopamine reward when they detect something that has not been fully predicted. Stories, moving at a faster pace than real life, and often through wider arcs of changes in fortune, invite us to make predictions yet continually outstrip what we can foresee. No wonder stories activate minds, command our attention, and offer us such intense rewards. Pure lyrics, lyrics without narrative, forfeit the predictions possible in terms of character and event, intention, action, and outcome, but they invite other predictions, even if often unconscious, in terms of word associations and line, rhythm, rhyme, and stanza structure.[27] We may expect a rhyme sound, but in a good poem we enjoy the unexpected, perhaps farfetched, move, and the unexpected word, that lead us to the right rhyme.[28]

Writers strive not only for novelty, for ways of keeping readers' reward systems alive by ensuring prediction errors. They also strive to reduce composition costs—by borrowing and recombining, where they can, ideas and devices that have worked for themselves or others—while maximizing composition benefits, by earning the most interest and the richest response from those readers they care to reach.[29] Readers, on the other hand, will prefer high comprehension benefits, low search costs, and comprehension costs as low as the high benefits they seek will allow. That will mean, for some, the pleasure of reading a familiar and therefore easy form, like rhymed poetry, different enough from everyday language to be worth special attention, but not greatly demanding, perhaps even as undemanding as greeting-card verse. For others it will mean searching for more novel language and ideas.

The competition for attention will lead poets both to invention, which can attract by novelty, and to the alternative, less costly in time and effort, the imitation of devices already known to secure attention by concentrating the patterns of the poetic line. What begins as innovation often turns into convention. The search for added impact, for instance, may distort normal usage in order to produce patterns with proven value in the verse line, such as, in English, inversion of the normal word order for the sake of rhythm and especially rhyme, long after the decline in grammatical inflections has reduced the flexibility of English word order. The quest for extra impact within the line, as in the eighteenth-century search for diction out of the ordinary—and for iambs—may even lead to clichéd poetic devices, like such fancy periphrases as "the feather'd quires" for *birds* or "the finny prey" for *fish*.

For some writers and readers, the establishment of conventions that seem to guarantee sufficient concentration for poetry will reduce search and comprehension time. For others, the attempt to amplify impact within existing modes will lead to highly patterned and highly charged poetry, making much of verse lines but at a cost too steep for many to wish to pay, thereby engendering what poet and critic James Longenbach calls "the resistance to poetry."[30] This repeatedly leads to reactions from poets who seek a fresh audience by challenging the innovations that have hardened into conventions, either too easy or too overloaded, and returning to an uncluttered, deconventionalized, perhaps more direct and more honest-seeming line.

Shakespeare adopts the conventions of the sonnet and the sonnet sequence, *and* challenges and refreshes them in ways that have earned wide and enduring attention, *and* charges them with so much pattern and so many surprises that they provoke in some lasting fascination and in others lasting exhaustion. Understanding just how and why he handles patterns and expectations and conventions should minimize the exhaustion and maximize the fascination.

2

Lyric and Sonnet

Verse minus Story: The Lyric

We all have a compulsive interest in others' actions and therefore in stories, real, fictional, or "reality show." But as we have seen, we have also evolved a craving for joint attention. Lyric verse invites us to share attention, wherever we are, even with a poet with no story to tell—or, more positively, a poet unconfined by story.

No chasm, of course, separates the continuous terrain of lyrical and narrative verse. Here I cannot avoid any longer defining narrative and its prototypical features, before turning to lyric. A narrative is *a representation of a coherent particular sequence of events, usually involving some agency and purpose.* An *event* (walking down to the shop, for instance) is not a narrative, any more

than an object (a cat, say) is a description. But just as a cat can become the object of a description, an event can become the subject
of a story, whether told in speech, writing, or images. A memory of
walking to the shop, or a dream of doing so, might *just* qualify as
a (private) narrative, although usually we use "narrative" to refer
to some explicit, potentially interpersonal representation: a gos-
sipy report to your neighbor, a diary entry (which somebody else
could see). A narrative would not usually be thought to consist of a
single event ("I got out of bed"), although any event can of course
be broken down into microevents (throwing aside the sheet, sitting
on the edge of the bed, putting my right foot on the floor . . .),
and conversely even a complex story can be summarized as a
single event (the story of the *Odyssey* could be compressed into
"Odysseus at last comes home"). Nor would a report of a mere
succession of disconnected events ("Joan of Arc was burnt at the
stake. In 1609 *Shake-speares Sonnets* was published. Yesterday my
car ran out of gas.") usually be thought to constitute a narrative,
although certain modern writers challenge the idea of a "coherent sequence of events" by, for instance, presenting unrelated
events (Barthelme's "The Indian Uprising"), undermining sequence (Robbe-Grillet's *Jealousy*), or minimizing events (Beckett).
But even in these radical instances, there is a kind of coherence
(paranoia, neurosis, paralysis, respectively) even in the incoher-
ence. A report of the weather for the day in a particular place
would be a representation of a coherent sequence of events, but
without agency and purpose we would not normally consider it a
narrative, although of course it could become the basis for a narrative by providing setting or circumstances for events about to
unfold. A report of my daily bus ride into work, my office and
class hours, my bus home, and so on has coherence, sequence,
agency, and purpose, but without a sense of the particular it
would seem a description of routine rather than a narrative.

Narrative may take many forms, but it is lyric that has been recognized as the most elusive to define of all literary genres[1]—if indeed, it should be seen as a genre and not as a mode or a mood. Nevertheless, most handbooks of literary terms accept lyric as nonnarrative, from M. H. Abrams's perennial *Glossary of Literary Terms* ("any fairly short, nonnarrative poem presenting a speaker who expresses a state of mind or a process of thought and feeling") to the recent *Handbook of Literary Terms* by poets X. J. Kennedy and Dana Gioia, and critic Mark Bauerlein ("now applies to any poem that focuses upon a speaker's feelings, as long as it doesn't veer into narrative"). Most critics accept the classical distinction between three literary modes, *epic* or *narrative* (the writer, poet or not, telling the story of the characters), *dramatic* (the writer, poet or not, embodying a story through the characters' speech), and *lyric* (the poet speaking in his or her own voice).

These are not rigid, neatly demarcated, nonintersecting sets. The boundaries can blur: two-thirds of both the *Iliad* and the *Odyssey* consist of dialogue; *The Prelude* is both epic and lyric, a story focused entirely on the poet speaking in his own voice and expressing his shifting thoughts and feelings. Lyrics can take dramatic form in, for instance, dialogues of self and soul; in dramatic monologues the speaker speaks in the first person, as in lyric, often addresses another, as in drama, and may not quite tell a story, as in narrative, but the poet-ventriloquist will have seen to it that a story can be inferred.

Nevertheless the three modes point to distinct tendencies and, in their prototypical forms, have distinct energies. In narratives, poets describe the characters from outside; in drama, characters speak for themselves; in lyric, poets or others speak in their own voice, often untrammeled by a narrative situation. Lyric poems need not exclude narrative, as a poem like Yeats's "Leda and the Swan" so wonderfully shows. Nor need they foreground the poet as a person. Emily Dickinson, famous for the resonant "I" that begins almost a hundred and fifty of her poems, can also leave herself quite out of the picture:

Who goes to dine must take his Feast
Or find the Banquet mean—
The Table is not laid without
Till it is laid within.

For Pattern is the Mind bestowed
That imitating her
Our most ignoble Services
Exhibit worthier.[2]

A key reason for the emphatic difference between lyric and both drama and narrative is that in the latter two, conflicts of will—or at least imperfect alignments of will, in, say, romantic comedy—tend to determine the flow. But in lyric, the poet or speaker can be free of such conflicts and may focus on herself or the world in any relation whatever and move in any direction. The poet may speak impersonally, as Dickinson does here, or personally, to herself, to one real or imagined other or to many others or to all comers, or to some part of her world, with any degree of passionate intimacy or relaxed openness.

The poet's potentially intense attention, line by line, free of any narrative pressure and therefore free to reflect on anything at all, and the reader's intense attention, line by line, create a compact between the poet potentially at her most private and unconstrained in subject and direction, and the reader at his most focused, ready to follow the unpredictable course of the poet's thoughts as suggested by the poet's words: a rare intimacy, across a great gap, between the poet at the moment of composition and the reader at the moment of reading. These two moments can be far apart in time and place but seem like the copresence of one free mind and another or others, totally focused, line by line.

The Loss of Story as the Gain of Lyric

Lyric poetry, like other mainly nonnarrative writing, cannot help—does not try to avoid—imagistic micronarratives.[3] Even the first sentence of my Introduction, "When did you last immerse yourself in a pool of make-believe?," incorporates a metaphorical mininarrative, albeit in the form of a question. And some poems that we regard as lyrics derive their force from mininarratives not far from metaphors. Dickinson's great death poems, like "I heard a fly buzz when I died" or "I felt a funeral in my brain," memorably establish narratives in their opening lines. While Shakespeare does not and could not avoid micronarratives, he does, I will try to show, eschew even mininarrative in his sonnets. Unlike other sonneteers of his time, he scrupulously avoids the defined sequences of event that characterize narrative as if to show what lyric poetry can achieve in the absence of story.

Normally joint attention connects us to something perceptually present or mutually known to be in focus ("mutually manifest," in Dan Sperber and Deirdre Wilson's terms).[4] But lyrics earn our attention even though they appeal to us when we are neither in the same physical or mental space as the poet nor transported into the shared concerns of a story. How?

First, by being verse, verse at full verve. Just as dogs perform play bows to solicit others to play fights or play chase, poets use the verse line and cues like rhythm, timing, rhyme, and unexpected images to solicit a play attitude to language. Not that play need mean unserious: just as physical play runs all the way from cavorting to chess and from backyard kickarounds to World Cups, the verbal play of lyrics ranges from nonsense verse to the elevation of elegy or ode. Especially in lyrics, without narrative to force an onward march, verse invites a special stance to language, inside a linguistic playground whose length and breadth are novelty of expression and richness of pattern. In his sonnets Shakespeare stretches both as far as he can.

Second, by being brief, without story to keep audiences asking "What next?" But lyrics, while they tend to forfeit sequential story, need not skirt situations: think of John Keats's "On First Reading Chapman's Homer" or Robert Frost's "Stopping by Woods on a Snowy Evening."[5] Shakespeare's sonnets in sequence make the most of the indefiniteness, the now-you-see-it-now-you-don't, of an intense emotional twosome or threesome sometimes emerging out of the shadows, sometimes perhaps still lurking in them, perhaps sometimes simply not there.

Third, by turning the absence of story to advantage. Lyric poetry allows us the illusion of access to another's thought at its least constrained by circumstance, in the very act of appealing to others regardless of *their* circumstances. Freedom from narrative allows thought to shape its own contexts and prompts.

Fourth, by the fertile indefiniteness of the act of utterance. In lyrics, poets may speak to themselves, or to specific others, even to intimate others, or to others in general, or they can speak as someone else, more or less implied or defined, in any of these roles. Poets can contemplate their own or other selves in isolation, or located in an immediate world, or in the most dramatic relation to others, or addressing us all, and can shift from one of these stances to another anywhere within the poem with a freedom unmatched elsewhere. Shakespeare turns this freedom to stunning emotional effect in the first of his sonnets we explore, in Chapter 3.

Fifth, by inviting an expansively resonating response. Since lyrics forfeit the supplied circumstances of a story, they need to appeal to *our* circumstances whatever these might be—and this usually means appealing to concerns connected with *any* reader's life. Sappho, Rumi, and Basho never imagined their poems affixed over subway or bus seats, but they would have been delighted to learn they could open up to readers even there. Poets work to achieve openness, especially by inviting openness in us. Lyrics carry an implicit invitation: whoever you are, whatever your circumstances, this concerns everyone, this concerns you. If you play the game, if you allow everything to resonate, you will hear how the images and ideas and emotions matter for us all.[6]

Sixth, by making the most of the tension between private thought in the making and the public finish of poetic form. Lyrics can seem on the one hand to offer immediate access to lone thought or intimate address and on the other to display all the self-consciousness and studiedness of literary art—as we will also see in the first Shakespeare sonnet we consider.

Seventh, by making brief but intense demands on attention. The best lyrics issue an immediate invitation to return to reread, to catch the uncaught, to savor the parts again in knowledge of the whole, "rereading," as Paterson observes, "being what is most distinct about the act of reading poetry."[7] Although, as in the case of Shakespeare's sonnets, lyrics often evoke the beauty of a thing, a moment, a thought, an experience, they also often express the ephemerality of their subjects. But unlike ever-changing life, they make it possible and inviting to return to the same experience, not diminished and blurred by memory but enriched by exact repetition, and at the same time enhanced by all the poem has already allowed us to discover and feel.

Lyric Freedom and Its Discontents

In narrative and drama, many kinds of pattern converge on the story elements: character (patterns of personality, role, affiliations, status, beliefs), plot (strategic social information, expectations, intentions, actions, reactions, outcomes), setting (physical and social), structures (plot and character contrasts, internal plot designs). These patterns tend not only to converge, but to be highly salient, the sorts that catch the attention of members of an ultra-social, highly cooperative, and highly competitive species such as ours. Lyric, which tends to deemphasize narrative, often turns to other kinds of patterns to catch our attention, and can have them converge—or not—according to criteria other than those that narrative automatically organizes.

The very freedom lyric can have from narrative offers opportunities and exacts costs. Because they can start and move anywhere, lyrics can often be highly exploratory, so much so that any potential defining term of lyric would only invite an ambitious poet to transgress the definition. (No wonder defining the lyric is so problematic!) Just as an Andy Goldsworthy can challenge the association of sculpture with the permanence of marble or bronze by creating sculptures not only in stone but also in flowing water, petals, and tide-washed ice, so a Walt Whitman can defy the expectation of brevity in lyric in the nearly two thousand lines of "Song of Myself."

The freedom of lyric also means that for the reader of a succession of unrelated lyrics, the comprehension costs of reorienting each time can be high. A different but related cost exists for the lyric poet. Because any starting point and any finishing point can be possible, and any course in between, the very freedom of lyric can open up a territory so unmarked as to paralyze choice. For that reason, lyric poets often alleviate the strain of freedom by following paths successfully broken by others: in terms of forms, like the sonnet, the quatrain, or the heroic couplet; in terms of set patterns, like end rhyme or alliterative hemistichs; in terms of set kinds of subject, like the love poem or song, or the elegy; and in terms, even, paradoxically, of set kinds of freedom, like the invitation to highly analogic thinking, such as metaphor and simile.

Precisely because of their freedom, lyrics embody a tension between the highly exploratory and the highly conventional. Devices that make the most of the concentrated attention that lyrics exact by deviating from normal expectations, will be used again by the same poet and others, and often become routinized into forms, conventions, and even clichés. In his sonnets Shakespeare accepts the sonnet form, with all its more or less fixed elements (line length, line number, metrical pattern, rhyme pattern), the sonnet sequence, with its predetermined subject of love, and sonnet imagistic conventions, of hyperbolic comparisons and favored content, such as eyes and hearts—but he also challenges every feature.

The Sonnet

The child's rhyme, when one hears another say words that happen to chime together, "You're a poet and you don't know it," speaks loudly of our pleasure in pattern, and of the salience of final sounds. But unlike lines, neither rhymes nor stanzas—fixed arrays of line patterns—are necessary to verse. Yet because we love pattern, rhyme and fixed stanzaic forms fill the oceans of verse like luminous sea creatures on dark tropical nights.

In European literatures, the sonnet has been by far the most successful of lyric verse forms. Emerging in twelfth-century Sicily, reaching a first climax in Petrarch in the fourteenth century, it reached another climax in the sixteenth and seventeenth centuries and has been continuously popular for the last two hundred years. One reason the sonnet has been such a success in such different settings is that it is short enough to attend to as a whole without losing focus and yet offers pattern of a complex and varied kind.

In the form of the sonnet that Petrarch favored, the fourteen lines divide into an octave, eight lines rhyming *abbaabba,* and then, usually after a *volta*—a turn of direction, a change in the movement of thought—a sestet, six lines with a pattern like *cd-ecde.* After first setting up expectations based on patterns of two, the sonnet shifts to a pattern of three, *cde,* just at the point where the vector of thought also usually veers. The switch of patterns, the momentary instability then recovered from by a different kind of pattern, *makes* the sonnet's magic.

Shakespeare did not invent, but did consistently adopt, another pattern, slightly less demanding in English—where words rhyme much less readily than in Italian[8]—but with no loss of patterned flexibility. In this pattern, with three sets of different alternating rhymes, *abab* (the first quatrain), *cdcd* (the second quatrain), *efef* (the third quatrain), and then *gg* (the closing couplet), the poet needs only two words to rhyme for each part of the pattern.

Just as the Petrarchan sonnet sets up a pattern in the octave, then breaks it in the sestet, so the Shakespearean sets up an even more emphatic pattern of alternating rhymes in the three quatrains, then breaks it in the adjacent rhymes of the couplet. That shift allows him to condense the rest of the sonnet, as it were, from twelve lines into two, into an emphatic closing epigram; or to advance just one stage further, to a clinching argument; or to take the thought to a new plane; or to turn the tables suddenly on the rest. On a first encounter we can never be sure whether the couplet will repeat, condense, advance, divert or reverse.

But Shakespeare also avails himself of another complication of the pattern of expectations. While the couplet always offers a shift of rhyme and reason, the sonnet in Shakespeare's hands can also introduce an earlier shift, at the point where the *volta* occurs in Petrarch: after line 8, after not an octave but two quatrains, and at the start of not a sestet but a third quatrain. So his sonnets may often work not with a 4+4+4 and-then-change-to-2 pattern

$(4+4+4+2)$, but as $4+4$, a pattern of eight, then change, $4+2$, a pattern of six, but within that, the last 2 lines still somehow changing in pace again: $(4+4)+(4+2)$. When he does not use that pattern, the three quatrains can provide different examples leading to the couplet's pithy conclusion, or an argument, over one quatrain or two, plus examples, over two quatrains or one. The quatrains can stand in parallel, or develop, or alternate in direction. Like the Petrarchan sonnet, the Shakespearean can divide into subunits of 1, 2, 3, 4, 6, 8, but in different ways, as wells as into a subunit of 12.

Sonnet structure allows a self-contained unit small enough to keep in mind at once, and a set of patterned expectations that build in variation within each sonnet but also offer variation from sonnet to sonnet. Despite the fixed patterns, and his making the most of the cues these patterns offer to him in writing and to us in reading, Shakespeare also plays with our expectations, keeping as a perpetual surprise just how thought or feeling will align with structure in any particular case. Surprise earns attention—as his sonnets continue to do.

3

A First Shakespeare Sonnet

Shakespeare's *Sonnets* constitute "arguably the most successful volume of poetry next to King David's Psalms."[1] I want us to consider how we, as modern readers, come to the sonnets, how Shakespeare led his original readers through the poems, and how we learn and appreciate more about them through reading again, or forward, or back, or around.

Most readers encounter their first Shakespeare sonnet, and may become interested in reading more, not in the context of the *Sonnets* as a collection but when a teacher, an anthologist, or a critic introduces them to one of the great sonnets. Sonnet 30, for instance:

When to the sessions of sweet silent thought
I summon up remembrance of things past,
I sigh the lack of many a thing I sought,

And with old woes new wail my dear time's waste;
Then can I drown an eye (unused to flow)
For precious friends hid in death's dateless night,
And weep afresh love's long-since-cancelled woe,
And moan th' expense of many a vanished sight;
Then can I grieve at grievances fore-gone,
And heavily from woe to woe tell o'er
The sad account of fore-bemoanèd moan,
Which I new pay as if not paid before.
   But if the while I think on thee (dear friend)
   All losses are restored, and sorrows end.[2]

Art needs to catch attention, and first impressions count, as psychologists confirm in experiments on what they call the primacy effect. No poet in English writes more attention-catching first lines than Dickinson ("Because I could not stop for death"), but Shakespeare, too, can catch us, even before sense crystallizes. The start of Sonnet 30 could be flatly expressed as "When I think fondly over the past." Shakespeare aims much higher.

Minds teem with expectations, most of them unconscious, all enabling us to make the most of the endless information "out there" in the limited mental space "in here." The usual needs little attention, and indeed nervous tissue, even in organisms as simple as sea slugs, habituates, or ceases to respond, to a continuous or repeated stimulus. As we learn a language we accumulate expectations about not only the sense of individual words and the structures of syntax but also the frequencies of sounds, words, ideas, and their likely combinations. Poems invite attention by playing with words in combinations that overturn expectation and therefore seize attention. A poem that began "When I think fondly over the past" might not entice anyone past the line break. A combination as full of surprise as "When to the sessions of sweet silent thought" makes our ears prick up, eager for more.

Part of the surprise comes from rhythm. In speech and prose we do not normally pay much heed to the pattern of syllabic stress. In the measured dose of a line of verse, we do. English speech and English verse tend to have a predominantly iambic (tee TUM tee TUM, "the CLOCK that TELLS the TIME") rhythm. English sonnets usually have an iambic pentameter meter, a template of five *tee TUMs* per line. A regular alternation of stressed and un-stressed syllables flows smoothly but becomes metronomically monotonic. Against the expectation of iambic pentameter, varia-tion stands out, and seems the more arresting—or, if taken too far, the more forced—the further it diverges from the norm. If we consider only *STRESSED* and *unstressed* syllables as options in each of the ten syllables in an iambic pentameter line, there is one option for a perfectly regular line and 1,023 other possible varia-tions ($2^{10} = 1,024$), some, of course, wildly more improbable than others. If we allowed for *half stresses,* and therefore three stress options per syllabic position, we could have 3^{10} or 59,049 possible combinations in each line.

"WHEN to the SES-sions of SWEET SI-lent THOUGHT" strikes us as an arresting variation on the iambic pentameter norm. Why? We do not really know. (Helen Vendler, perhaps the finest writer alive on English verse, mostly refuses to discuss meter in her brilliant book on Shakespeare's sonnets because, she says, we lack "an acceptably subtle and yet communicable theory of scansion.")[3] There is nothing inherently arresting about line 1's *TUM tee tee TUM tee tee TUM TUM tee TUM* sequence except that when "*tee TUM* x 5" is the norm this is decidedly not "same old" or "ho HUM" x 5.

The abstract pattern cannot be considered apart from meaning and sound.[4] Think of human faces as an analogy. Any human understands the template of a human face—forehead, brows, two forward-facing eyes with whites, ridged nose, widish mouth with lips, chin—and even day-old infants look longer at a circular array with two small circles sufficient to suggest eyes than at similar but not facelike configurations. We can instantly distinguish one human face from another, and a beautiful or a striking face from an ugly or forgettable one; but in most cases we cannot explain how the size, shape, position, and color of the individual elements, and their combination, their symmetry and their closeness to the norm, shape the individual impression or account for its appeal. In the same way we can be aware intuitively or explicitly of the metrical template and hear the stresses that the actual syllables in a line need, but not know why the combination of sounds, words, phrases, and emerging sense and feeling and their variations from the template seem to dance, strut, or stumble.

In the first line of Sonnet 30 the echo of the same vowel sound in the first two stressed syllables, in "WHEN to the SESsions of," somehow adds to the smooth but forceful flow of the verse feet. The change in pace from the speed of the first six syllables, two stresses out of six syllables, to the slowing down in the last four syllables, three stresses out of four, strikes us (strikes me, anyway: I have to assume that I am a normal Anglophone animal) as a pleasing change in tempo. The successive stresses in "SWEET SI-lent" almost enforce an ensuing pause that makes us linger over the special qualities of the "THOUGHT." And the whole line runs with a confidence—quite unlike "When I think fondly over the past"—that makes us feel when we reach "I summon" in the next line that these words have indeed been summoned with aplomb.

None of these effects will be registered consciously without the kind of deliberate analysis here (lengthened, alas, with background explanation). We just find a line surprising and pleasing against our intuitive expectations of English word choice and rhythm. I expect neurocognitive research to help work out why, although it is already clear that thought is in many ways embodied, that words even when read silently activate the motor cortex to some extent as if we were uttering the words aloud, and that mental activity depends on the rhythmic synchronization of firing neurons. Somehow great poets in their best lines maximize the variation, pacing, and patterning of stress and sequence in ways that generate instant interest and conviction.

As we read the first line of Sonnet 30, we accept a down payment of sense and an immediate reward in its fresh confident configuration. That's easily enough to engage us. Over the next few lines the emerging sense and situation and the rich mood of retrospective sorrow add more lures for the hook of attention, still kept sharp line by line with verbal surprises like "And with old woes new wail my dear time's waste." Although we can understand anything routine almost without reflection, divergences from the norm like this line, while they arouse more interest, require more effort to absorb. Yet Shakespeare has a knack of allowing us, most of the time, to catch the gist, even if exact decoding eludes our grasp, a quick whiff of sense along with the complex surprise of the taste.[5] At the same time he erects helpful signposts and rest-stops to mark the emotional and imaginative route of each sonnet, in this case "When . . . I . . . ," starting the first quatrain, "Then can I . . . ," starting the second and the third, "But if . . ." introducing the last-minute turn that sends the poem soaring.

This famous sonnet sets the pleasures of memory against its pains, the balm of recollection against the astringent recognition that what we can reach only by recalling, we cannot have at hand. In statement, but not in effect, the poem could be condensed to: "When I think over the past, I grieve anew at all I have lost, but if I think of thee, dear friend, all losses are restored, and sorrows end." What makes this one of Shakespeare's greatest sonnets is that after its elaborations, after its long retrospectives of sorrow, even in the sweet backcast of memory, there comes, but only at the very end, the surprise of its final shift: a speaker who had seemed alone with his losses suddenly has a dear friend to address, who dispels all this reminiscential grief. Final impressions matter too: as psychologists show, what they call the recency effect shapes our conclusions and therefore our mood. The relief here, after the refrains of regret, floods the sonnet's darkness with a sudden illumination that transforms its emotional world and our grasp of its sense and shape.

Successful works of art of different kinds invite different kinds of responses. A long narrative can build its impact slowly over time, creating its own internal tensions and resolutions, and leave a long aftereffect. A successful short lyric, like a sonnet, over quickly, invites us back to resavor it immediately, turning it around in the mind's grasp, as we might slowly revolve a gem to watch the play of light and shape on each facet. A great lyric can hold the attention not only of many readers over many centuries but of many responsive readers over many repeated readings.

We can express this in terms of costs and benefits. A brief lyric will often risk raising costs of comprehension line by line in order to maximize the verbal and structural patterns that can attract our attention and lock in the impact of patterns of idea or emotion, in a form in which patterns of character and event have too little time to develop. At the end of a good lyric, we savor the effect of completion, the match between sense and shape, and we usually return to savor the patterns again, conscious now how they resolve themselves, and to see if our knowledge of the developing sense can illuminate incidental obscurities.

Psychology shows that we can take in more information when anxiety levels drop: "Research suggests that people in positive and playful moods are more open to experience and learn in better and in more varied ways."[6] Tracking through a new poem, confronted with its verbal intensity, uncertain where it will lead, we can often feel a measure of apprehension that inhibits comprehension. As we return to a Shakespeare sonnet, now aware of the poem's direction, appreciative of what it has already offered and eager to catch more, we can usually disentangle its occasional difficulties, or enjoy their suspension between different, mostly concordant, resolutions. We can linger over a phrase like "And with old woes new wail my dear time's waste" and see that its last four words, for instance, could mean "the waste or loss of things that have been dear to me over time" or "my wasting my time, which should have been precious to me, not doing the things I should have done in a time that I can't have back." In this typical Shakespearean risk-taking compression we can see that he packs words together in ways we can't quite unpack one at a time, yet the overall sense tumbles out, the different possible decodings overlap and largely converge.[7]

As cognitive psychology has demonstrated, human attention has tight limits, about seven or fewer chunks of information at once. A ten-syllable verse line like Shakespeare's may just exceed this, with the first half of the line coming in to clear mental focus ("And with old woes new wail") just as the second half demands attention ("my dear time's waste"), but with the three-second auditory present allowing our mind's ear to replay the first half, already mentally processed, as we encounter the second.

We attend to the patterns of local sense, at the level of the line and the sentence, and to the emerging global sense of the sonnet. We may also note on first exposure the most prominent patterns, like alliterations and rhymes (the onsets and endings of words are particularly salient, and *line* endings more so still, thanks to the blank line-end in print or the extra beat on the last syllable, even in a run-on line, made by a good verse speaker). But other patterns will tend to elude attention when we first read, and to emerge and

offer new pleasure as we reread with more attention to spare. In
the hands of a great poet, patterns interlaced with other patterns,
or patterns hidden behind patterns, turn rereading a poem into a
game of hide-and-seek.

Unlike many other Shakespeare sonnets, Sonnet 30 almost ignores the visual and the figurative. Instead, the poet saturates
his poem with patterns of sound. And although he does demarcate structure, sense, and syntax, he does not markedly differen-
tiate the subject from quatrain to quatrain: each quatrain shows
the speaker sunk in the repetitions of grief, as if Shakespeare
needs time to accumulate the apparent monotony of grief before suddenly dismissing it. Within and between quatrains, he
amasses phonic repetitions: the *s*'s and *w*'s of quatrain 1, the "silent thought . . . sigh . . . sought" echoed by quatrain 2's "sight," the
"thought . . . thing . . . thing . . . sought" echoed in the couplet's
"think," and the first line's "si*l*ent *thought*" answered in the penul-
timate line's "wh*ile* I *think*." Quatrain 2's "pre*ci*ous . . . a*fresh*"
meshes with the first quatrain's "se*ssi*ons." In the tour de force of
quatrain 3, each line accentuates the repetition of griefs through the
repetition of sound, but in a different way each time—"moan . . .
many," "grieve at grievances," "woe to woe," and "fore-bemoaned
moan"—but the "*fore*- . . . *o'er* . . . *fore*- . . . be*fore*" pattern finds
its requital in the last line's "rest*ore*d." And after the round of
seemingly relentless repetition of word and sound, in the last line,
suddenly, every word save "and" is new.

The patterns need not be only of sound, and since we do not
know quite what we will find, we tend to follow one search cue at
a time. In Sonnet 30 vivid visual images may be lacking, but not
images altogether. Legal imagery featured often enough in Early
Modern sonnets to be parodied,[8] but here Shakespeare quietly
evokes the idea of court sessions in line 1 and quietly strengthens it
in line 2's "summon." In line 7 he begins another pattern of sub-
dued images, here of accounting or reckoning, both activated by

the sense of losses that starts with line 3's "lack" and reaching back to "sessions" and "summon," as if to introduce "the idea of a courtroom of fiscal enquiry, where all the losses on one side of the ledger are balanced by the existence of the Friend":[9] "dear," "waste," "precious," "long-since-cancelled woe" (as if a woe were a debt), "expense," "tell o'er / The sad account" ("tell" in the sense of "count up," as a bank teller still does), "pay . . . paid," "losses are restored."

If the images of "a kind of emotional stocktaking"[10] subtly bind the poem together, and reinforce the consistency and persistence of morose memorial delectation, syntax here offers us still another layer of pattern that marks the key disruption in the poem. We usually think of verbs as concrete, but this sonnet swarms with verbs, almost all with the speaker as subject, that remain abstract or at least unimagistic, registering not so much action as emotion. The first thirteen lines have eleven finite verbs, all with *I* as subject (summon, sigh, sought, wail, can drown, weep, moan, can grieve, tell, pay, think). But once the speaker, seemingly isolated in retrospective sorrows, thinks of the unexpected "thee (dear friend)," *I* drops out as subject, and two new subjects in the sonnet's last line reverse the poem's entire direction: "All losses are restored, and sorrows end."

Art needs to attract attention fast, but great art attracts it again and again. Returning to reread a lyric can be a rich and multilayered experience. With the first reading fresh in our minds, with the text there as a series of fixed and exact prompts to memory, we can both relive and reconstruct our initial impressions—except that we can also now be aware of what we have already understood, and no longer have the anxiety we felt on a first exploration—and augment them. We can "chunk" some of the sense we have already grasped, hold it in mind as a unit, to allow us more mental space to attend to other features, like new kinds of pattern or emotion or idea. We can enjoy the initial pleasure again—and its

being still available for re-enjoyment amplifies the first response—
but we can also appreciate each phrase and phase for the way it
develops ideas, emotions, and patterns we now know emerge during the poem. We can see how Shakespeare has both shaped ap-
peals to first-time readers and overloaded the lines so that rereaders can extract still more point and pattern.

On a first exposure we will be likely to have noticed, for instance, the alliterations in line 4, since alliterations are naturally
cognitively salient, and since here they are so abundant: "And
*w*ith old *w*oes new *w*ail my dear time's *w*aste." We may have been
too anxious to grasp the sense behind the odd phrasing to linger
over the other patterns on our first encounter, but when we return, especially after we have "chunked" the sense of "my dear
time's waste," we will be able to focus on additional patterns, like
the assonance (the repeated vowel sounds, slightly less salient because in the middle of the words, and because here spelled differently) of "w*ai*l" and "w*a*ste." Or, more complexly: "old" and "new"
are among the most obvious contrasting pairs in English or any
other language, but Shakespeare takes the old and makes it new
by ramming these up against each other, "old woes new wail," and
by having each of them modify a word in *w,* and using "old" in its
old sense as an adjective, but "new" in a new way and a new position, as an adverb and unexpectedly and un-Englishly (but that's
never bothered Shakespeare) before the verb.[11] (Largely because of
the foregrounded verbal pattern in the sonnets, as opposed to the
plays, Shakespeare uses "new," often in pointed contrast with
"old," twice as often per line in the sonnets as in the plays.)[12]

Recently psychologists have investigated the mind's capacity to
metarepresent, to understand representations *as* representations:
to comprehend a picture or report or memory as *of* a place or a

time, say, or an attitude, one's own or another's, as *to* something. Most psychologists link metarepresentation with Theory of Mind, the capacity to understand our own mental states and to infer those of others, and see both as emerging from our intense sociality.[13] As ultrasocial creatures we have evolved to cope easily with four or sometimes five orders of intentionality, with Golda's amusement at Jane's scorn at Bruce's fears about Helen's attraction to Richard.[14] Returning to a poem, we can hold in mind (and partly reconstruct: memory is constructive, not eidetic) our first-time response and label it as past, while enjoying new discoveries, and infer *here* the poet's intentions to elicit the initial response or *there* to pack in more for rereaders to unpack. We can turn our social-cognitive Theory of Mind and metarepresentational skills onto our own response, and the responses of other readers we imagine, and the poet's intentions in eliciting these responses for us, for his and our likes. Evolutionary social psychologists have also discovered the unique speed and efficiency of our physical and emotional attunement to one another, and the strength of our disposition to share attention with others.[15] These, too, amplify our response.

In any artistic mode understanding depends to some extent on expertise built up by repeated exposure and/or explicit instruction, effects that psychologists have studied specifically in the appreciation of poetry.[16] Yet the echo chamber of the mind, which amplifies present response by bouncing the speaker's expressed experiences, emotions, and ideas off the walls of our own remembered responses, the imagined responses of others, and the inferred intentions of the author to elicit all these, is part of our normal neural architecture. And we all have a predilection for pattern. While the resonance of response can be damped down by anxiety, it can be readily released, for anyone who understands the poem's language, through experience, time, guidance, and a stress-free reading situation.

In the case of "When to the sessions of sweet silent thought," for instance, we enjoy the poet's evocation of the ample sorrows of remembrance—sorrows, yet also a measure of the accumulated riches of what he has experienced—and the chords his words strike in our own experience or, as we imagine, all human experience. We may particularly enjoy the relief of the sudden recollection of the friend whose evocation displaces all the sorrows with joy. As we reread, we appreciate the poet's care with sound and syntax to magnify the sense of the oppressive repetitiveness of experiences and memories of loss, and the economy and magnitude of the shift in the final couplet. If we have read enough to know the specifics of Shakespeare's usual handling of the sonnet, we will notice that the "When . . . Then . . . Then" at the start of the three quatrains, rather than some change at the start of the third quatrain, itself emphasizes the onerous repetitiveness of melancholy reminiscence in the first twelve lines; if we know his habitual shift in pace and often in attitude in the couplet, we will also recognize that no other couplet change is so extreme in mood and manner as this, with the last-minute introduction of the addressee, the sudden lift in spirits, the sudden switch in syntax and vocabulary.

While we could note such patterns as merely objectively present, our minds are not made to see them that way. We have not an instinctive but, as mature users of a language, a highly automatic capacity for understanding the probabilities of patterns in our language(s), even if often we could not articulate our sense of normal expectations until we see or hear them violated. We recognize the pains Shakespeare must have taken to maximize the patterns of repetition in the three quatrains, and to keep the multiple measures of difference in reserve for the closing couplet, and we cannot help inferring intentions behind such deliberateness—to express to the fullest the speaker's sorrow and to infect readers' minds with a matching emotion, and then to recreate in writer and readers the magic of the mood change on recalling the "dear friend." Our minds have been shaped to understand others in terms of intentions, in terms of their deliberate actions, and to respond to them accordingly. Understanding the care with which Shakespeare has shaped the sonnet, and overloaded it with patterns that influence us from the start but that offer us more than we can assimilate at once, so as to allow a gradual sustained release of pleasure in rediscovering the creative magic of his choices, amplifies our response in ways that we as humans have been made to find deeply moving and deeply exciting. As tireless appraisers of one another, we appreciate Shakespeare's exceptional skill and his generosity in taking such pains to prepare for us such pleasure at unpacking his imaginative gift.

Even if we don't yet know the structural patterns Shakespeare habitually exploits throughout his sonnets, we can continue to explore local patterns that emerge under our attention. The "woes" in "with old woes new wail" in the last line of the first quatrain returns in the second quatrain, "weep afresh love's long since cancelled woe" (with, again, alliteration on the *w* as well as, this time, on *l* and on the *s* and *ns* sounds of "*s*in*ce*" and "ca*n*celled"); and then again, twice, in the third quatrain, alliterating with itself: "heavily from *w*oe to *w*oe tell o'er." Repeatedly in the playful patterning of the sonnets Shakespeare picks out words from his immense vocabulary and bounces them through as many hoops as he can find.

And his patterns seem to have purpose behind the playfulness. All the words in the last line except "and," as we have seen, are new. The second-to-last word is "sorrows," which picks up on the emphatic *s* alliteration in the opening "sessions of sweet silent thought," and with its final syllable, "-ows," rhymes with the "woe" in each quatrain. It has the *s* of "woes" in the first quatrain, but declares that these "sorrows," which had seemed so endlessly repeated, now suddenly *end* because he thinks of his *friend.* That "-ows" sound of *sorrows* picks up on "woes" but flips it around and brings it to an end, the way remembering his friend suddenly puts a stop to his woes.

Or to take a simpler pattern, but also one not likely to be noticed on a first reading. The sounds and semantic links of "sweet s*IL*ent *TH*ought" in the poem's opening line will be subtly echoed in the opening line of the countermovement in the closing couplet, "if the wh*IL*e I *TH*ink." "Thought" in the first line is a noun, but inevitably and intimately tied to *thought,* the past tense of the verb *think.* In this sonnet saturated with thought and with verbs, the verb *think* does not occur until the key action, the great surprise of the poem, at the start of the couplet: "But if the while I think on thee." Despite the expectations set up by "sweet" in the first line, the "silent thought" throughout the three quatrains has proved much closer to bitter than to sweet, but the last-minute "if the while I think on thee, dear friend" suddenly explains why the speaker can call his musings "sweet": because they are, once his dear friend comes to mind.

Not all readers will see or search for all these patterns, although readers with the curiosity to return, and the confidence to embark again on the voyage of rediscovery, will find these and more.[17] But if it takes expertise with poems or at least with this particular poem to respond to *all* its intricate artistry, to its deliberate shaping, to the particular effects of *this* work, readers can also respond more immediately to the individual tang of the poet's voice. Our expectations of the norms of English, even if only intuitive and implicit rather than readily articulated, quickly alert us to divergences from the easy and habitual.

Shakespeare's bold individuality with the language probably strikes us from the first, and proves instantly attractive, but we need to return, to slow down, to see just how strange it is. In line 3, for instance, "I sigh the lack of many a thing I sought," "sigh the lack" is an oddity: *sigh* with a direct object. In English we usually sigh *for;* poets can even sigh words, breath, notes, proverbs (three of these instances, the earliest in the *OED,* are Shakespeare's); but Shakespeare is the first to use "sigh" with a direct object that has nothing to do with utterance, but only with the object, the thing sighed for. If other writers follow his lead, they have tamer, more obvious objects for "sigh": "sigh my funeral" (Marston) or "sigh her fate" (Prior). But Shakespeare compounds the strangeness by making the direct object not a single word but a noun clause, "the lack of many a thing I sought." Here the apparently plain, unpoetic "thing" in fact picks up elegantly on "remembrance of things past" in the previous line, and *sought* oddly chimes with *sigh,* as if, Helen Vendler comments, the second verb were the past tense of the first.[18] Readers may not notice or have the vocabulary or have done the lexical research to explain all the oddness here, but *any* fluent reader of English will sense the divergence from modern usage in "sigh the lack," and anyone attuned to late Elizabethan English will sense the bold Shakespearean flouting of the norms. In the next line, "And with old woes new wail my dear time's waste," we have already commented on the compounding compression of "my dear time's waste," the almost jarring juxtaposition, here, of *old* and *new,* and the placement of *new* as an adverb and before the verb, but even the verb itself is odd. *Wail* with a direct object is not as unprecedented as *sigh* used the same way, but with a compound and echoing direct object, "wail my dear time's waste," it violates English norms in several directions, and all the more so when we also note the strangeness of the construction "wail . . . with woes."

Shakespeare's contemporary John Donne strives for effect in similes as striking as his famous comparison between, on the one hand, lovers parting yet still linked and, on the other, the legs of a compass, or in outbursts as dramatic as "Batter my heart, three-person'd God." The mature Shakespeare by contrast seems simply unable not to express himself, especially within the constrained concentration of the sonnets, in ways that overstep the borders of English, foot by foot. Donne advertises his originality; Shakespeare exudes his from every verbal pore.

Among the pleasures of great art is our sense of contact with individual artistic minds. All the same the individuality we sense in verbal art seems especially uncanny, since usage stamps words out uniformly, precisely so that each verbal coin has the same value in any hand and can therefore be readily exchanged as the unquestioned currency of thought. Shakespeare in this sonnet engages us by appealing to the commonness of human experience and emotion, and in words standard in English, but he combines these words in ways that manifest his individuality, his quiet boldness, his instinctive, incessant originality along so many axes, line after line.

That originality pervades his plays, too. But we can deepen our sense of the intentions in his sonnets by thinking of his artistic problem situation[19] in writing sonnets rather than plays.[20] Here in Sonnet 30 Shakespeare expresses the repetition of remembered woe and the restoration that present friendship allows not only in idea but also in the patterns of word, sound, image, and structure. These patterns would draw unwelcome attention to themselves in drama but perfectly suit the sonnet's capacity to concentrate attention on a line, a quatrain, or a whole poem at once. Here as elsewhere in his best sonnets, Shakespeare makes the poem in part a hide-and-seek game, and therefore very different from the verse in his plays. There, characters who spoke in a sonnet as tightly patterned as this would sound highly artificial, and in any case most of the effects would be lost on audiences without the time to focus attention as closely as a sonnet-reader can. Here in the sonnets Shakespeare does not try to sound natural—although he tries to make the *feelings* natural—but to crank up what he says to the utmost. And as in all his sonnets, he plays instinctively with our minds' innate inclination to look for pattern, on the one hand, and on the other with our inevitable difficulty of knowing *when* we have found a significant or signifying pattern amid so much information.

From Sonnet to Sequence

4

Love

The Mistress

After encountering a few of the greatest sonnets one at a time, modern readers may be tempted to turn to the sonnets as a whole. They often find themselves taxed, disappointed, and perplexed. Shakespeare's *Sonnets* may be the most successful collection of secular lyrics in at least the Western tradition, but readers far more often begin the volume than end it. The sequence can be demanding line by line and sonnet by sonnet, and it remains famously riddling as a whole.

The most successful works of art, like Shakespeare's greatest sonnets, can and often do stand on their own. More problematic cases often need an explanation of their background. To understand the *Sonnets* as a collection I think we need the deep background of evolution as well as the immediate background of Shake-speare's work and world.

Shake-speares Sonnets starts with sperm trying to meet eggs— and not just with John Shakespeare's meeting Mary Arden's. "Re-ductive," you might think. Or "*Eggs?* What about the Fair Youth?" Wait and see.

Shake-speares Sonnets

All Shakespeare's known sonnets, except those embedded in his plays, were published together in 1609. Scholars still debate whether the book advertised on its title page and throughout the volume as *Shake-speares Sonnets* was prepared by Shakespeare, or at least approved by him, or whether it was pirated and printed without his knowledge and overseeing. Scholars still do not agree when in his compact literary career he wrote the poems, whether he wrote them in a single sustained effort, or in several such ef-forts, or more or less piecemeal, and only afterward placed them in the sequence we now have, or whether indeed it was he who determined their order. One index of the challenge the sonnets' sequence poses is that over the last two centuries many have tried to reorder them, usually "to create a more intelligible 'story,' "[1] but no new sequence has won general acceptance.

Nevertheless, evidence about order and date has accumulated and converged over the last half-century. The majority of those who have worked most intensely on the sonnets have moved from the earlier consensus that they were amassed and printed by an unscrupulous and piratical publisher to the conclusion that the whole volume, sequence and all, was designed by Shakespeare to work within, against, and around the convention of sonnet se-quences so popular in England in the early 1590s (see especially the work of MacDonald P. Jackson and of Katherine Duncan-Jones).[2]

Recent evidence also shows it is unlikely that, as once thought, Shakespeare wrote all his sonnets in the early years of his career. He now appears to have written some in the mid-1590s, others late in the decade, and still others up until about 1604. He may well have continued to revise until shortly before publication, and seems to be responsible for the final order.[3]

Love, Sonnets, and Sexual Selection

Since Shakespeare's time, poets have written sonnets on many subjects, from John Milton's "On His Blindness" and Keats's "On First Reading Chapman's Homer," to Carol Ann Duffy's dramatic monologues ("Human Interest," a knife-killer's lament; or "Anne Hathaway," a surprising view from that second-best bed—of which, more later). But Shakespeare's initial audience thought of sonnets, most often, as love poems.

One of the readiest evolutionary explanations for sonnets, or for any of the arts, is sexual selection. The logic of reproductive specialization into female and male leads to one sex's producing resource-rich eggs and the other's producing massive numbers of cheap but highly motile sperm to increase the chance that some will reach the far fewer available eggs. Sperm is cheap and eggs are dear: one man produces enough new sperm every month to fertilize in theory every woman of reproductive age in the world.[4] Not only do females produce vastly fewer eggs than males, but once an egg is fertilized, they may have to commit weeks or months to its gestation. Females therefore have reason to be highly selective in accepting males as partners. As a result males need to compete against one another for females, and do so either head to head, literally, like stags and stag beetles, by knocking out the competition, or, as it were, head to heart, by competing to appeal to the available females more than other males do. In this latter case males need to display—to demonstrate their desirability to females, in the hope of being selected by at least one of them. In many species in which intersexual selection operates, that can lead to the hypertrophy of a single suite of features, like the peacock's tail or the male bowerbird's compulsion to build bowers taller and more tasteful than those of his rivals. In the human world, where we have discovered the power of specialization, there may be many routes to success and therefore many avenues for male display. Among those we prize most are the intellectual and the creative, and their combination. Steven Pinker makes the case vividly: "the impulse to create art is a mating tactic: a way to impress prospective sexual and marriage partners with the quality of one's brain and thus, indirectly, one's genes. Artistic virtuosity . . . is unevenly distributed, neurally demanding, hard to fake, and widely prized. Artists, in other words, are sexy."[5] Today young male comics artists frequently explain their art as a way to attract young women who might otherwise ignore them as physically unprepossessing or socially unconfident.

Although males produced far more sonnets in the English Renaissance than did women,[6] and the same holds for rap music now, sexual selection seems a woefully insufficient explanation for art, especially when both sexes engage in art long before puberty and long after peak reproductive years and when art can serve communal and even religious functions. As I write elsewhere, sexual selection may provide an extra gear for art, but not its engine.[7] Even if sexual selection amplifies male artistic energy, especially in public art, the drive need not be consciously linked with sex. Yet at the end of the sixteenth century sonnets were insistently, comically, associated with love and male pursuit. In what may be Shakespeare's first comedy, *The Two Gentlemen of Verona,* Proteus urges Thurio:

You must lay lime, to tangle her desires
By wailful sonnets, whose composed rhymes
Should be full-fraught with serviceable vow. . . .   (III.2.69–71)

In *Much Ado about Nothing,* Claudio produces the proof that
Benedick loves Beatrice:

And I'll be sworn upon't that he loves her,
For here's a paper written in his hand,
A halting sonnet of his own pure brain,
Fashion'd to Beatrice.

Hero continues:

And here's another
Writ in my cousin's hand, stol'n from her pocket,
Containing her affection unto Benedick. (V.4.85–90)[8]

Shakespeare has Romeo and Juliet signal their perfect suitedness
in love from the start by exchanging their first words in sonnet
form. And in the *Sonnets* themselves, in his proudest boast of the
immortality of his verse, Sonnet 55, "Not marble nor the gilded
monuments," Shakespeare concludes: "So, till the judgment that
yourself arise, / You live in this, and dwell in lovers' eyes." Lovers,
he assumes, form the natural readership for sonnets.

Sonnet 1 . . . 45

Shakespeare's own surviving sonnets appear to have begun with
an instance of pure sexual selection: with a Stratford teenager appealing to a Stratford twenty-something by writing her a sonnet,

the very type of the love poem in their time. Although Shakespeare, as coy about self-disclosure as ever, did nothing to announce it, he has allowed readers to deduce—eventually!—that Sonnet 145 was written for Anne Hathaway.

Composed in iambic tetrameter rather than the normal iambic pentameter, with a much thinner texture than the other sonnets, and conspicuously different from its neighbors in tone, content, and imagery, Sonnet 145 was often considered of doubtful authenticity. But it has now been recognized as a wooing sonnet, a male display of playful intelligence:

> Those lips that love's own hand did make,
> Breathed forth the sound that said "I hate"
> To me that languished for her sake;
> But when she saw my woeful state,
> Straight in her heart did mercy come,
> Chiding that tongue, that ever sweet
> Was used in giving gentle doom,
> And taught it thus anew to greet:
> "I hate" she altered with an end
> That followed it as gentle day
> Doth follow night, who, like a fiend,
> From heaven to hell is flown away.
> > "I hate" from hate away she threw,
> > And saved my life, saying "not you."

As Andrew Gurr first noticed in 1971, and as almost all commentators have accepted since, "hate away" in line 13 puns on "Hathaway." The whole sonnet labors rather creakily to reach the reversal delayed until the closing couplet: if "she" agrees to accept his suit, she throws her "hate" away along with her "Hathaway" name (in Shakespeare's day *th* could often be pronounced as *t*, as in the pun on "noting" in the title of *Much Ado about Nothing*), while in this context "And" in the next line puns on "Anne": "*Anne* saved my life" by turning her "hate" away into love.[9] Evidently the sonnet itself, or the creative intelligence it required for a young man to compose such a thing, worked: Will Shakespeare appealed to Anne Hathaway enough to win access to her, to marry her, to have children by her. Desire, nature's "proximate mechanism," allowed Will S. and Anne H. to reproduce, to fulfill nature's "ultimate function," to beat death in nature's way.

We can easily see Sonnet 145 as Shakespeare's own "halting sonnet" of *his* pure young brain, from its first weakly similar *abba* rhymes (make/hate/sake/state), through its insipid diction and its flabby filler, to its mundane comparison, "as gentle day / Doth follow night." Yet if Shakespeare was only eighteen at the time, he had already mastered sonnet structure enough to toy with it. A sonnet's *volta,* its switch or turn in thought, if present, usually comes at the start of line 9. At that point here, the woman's second "I hate" teasingly echoes the "I hate" at the start of the poem, as if to repeat rather than rebuff the initial danger. In fact the countermovement has already begun, unusually early indeed, with the "But" starting the last line of the first quatrain. Yet line 2's "hate" still reverberates, and at the start of line 9, in the place of the usual *volta,* it seems to have recurred, even if these very words will end by saving the poet-lover, at the last possible moment, when we reach the final two words of the poem. (As we have seen, Sonnet 30 plays, much more subtly, on the last-minute reprieve.) Like Shakespeare's inventiveness of structure, the fondness for contrasts that saturates his mature sonnets ("with old woes new wail," "Fairing the foul," "Love is my sin, and thy dear virtue hate") also announces itself already here, in "day-night," "heaven-hell," and especially in the charm of the contrast between "love" and "hate" that shapes the whole poem.[10]

Beyond Sexual Selection

But not even the young Shakespeare's efforts, at eighteen or so, could reach great heights. Until the playful allusions to "Hathaway" and "Anne" were noted in print almost four hundred years later, Sonnet 145 had often been considered non-Shakespearean, because so evidently inferior in quality and complexity to the much maturer remainder. Sexual selection can explain neither Shakespeare's eventual high achievements as a sonneteer nor the particular form he chose to work within. While ardent Elizabethan youths may have written sonnets as love poems, the sonnet *sequences* that became so popular in England in the 1580s and 1590s were less the product of youthful ardor than of specialized craft by poets highly informed by literary tradition—although that impulse to achieve status through specialization might well itself incorporate an element of sexual selection.

Specialization

As a species we have long established an economy of surplus through trade and exchange, dependent on specialization, which allows individuals to benefit by producing goods or developing skills that others do not have.[11] Just as others assess us, including members of the opposite sex, we readily appraise ourselves against others and from early in life choose niches of comparative competence[12]—as Shakespeare did, with Anne Hathaway in the 1580s and London in the 1590s, in trusting to his talents as a writer.

Men have on average a stronger desire than women for status,[13] partly because status can mean better access to scarce resources, including the special biological resource of females' reproductive capacity. (The link between status and access to females, while it may be conscious—think Silvio Berlusconi—need not be.) That sexual element, recognized or not, can help motivate the practice that even talent needs in order to attain singular achievement.

Practice itself has features of a subsidiary Darwinian process: a cycle of many trials, starting from imitation of the successes of others, then from positions reached by one's own best successes in previous rounds—a process that therefore allows for the accumulation over time of more complex successes.[14] Just as the repeated rounds of natural selection can accentuate differences between organisms that once belonged to the same species, so practice can greatly accentuate individual differences in performance.

Social Selection

But the motivation for the extreme training necessary for exceptional human achievement is less specifically *sexual* selection than the wider mechanism of *social* selection: not selection just of males by females, as in peacocks or bowerbirds, but, in our ultra-social species, selection by all, or by those whose approval matters most.

As Darwin reflected: "Even when we are quite alone, how often do we think with pleasure or pain of what others think of us,—of their imagined approbation or disapprobation; and this all follows from sympathy, a fundamental element of the social instincts."[15] Recent findings on the power of human empathy, attunement, joint attention, and Theory of Mind extend his insight. We humans have a unique and deep desire—one we normally take for granted but extraordinary among all other forms of life we know—to imagine the thoughts and feelings of others.[16] More than any other mode of art, lyric poetry invites us to dwell on the intimate and untrammeled thoughts and feelings of another "even when we are quite alone."

The Sonnet Sequence: Biology and Culture

"Every man and woman alive today," writes Paul Seabright in his *The War between the Sexes*, "has emotions and perceptions that are shaped by the simple asymmetry between sperm and eggs."[17] In most animal species, males, with sperm to spare, compete to be selected by females, with their limited supply of eggs and therefore with much more reason than males to be choosy. In many monogamous species, in which male assistance in the rearing of offspring regularly raises their survival rates, females become still more selective in choosing long-term mates. In such species females seek, and males need to provide, proof of commitment. Females can test male commitment best by resistance, by making would-be partners demonstrate their persistence.

In the human case the sexual imbalance between minimum male and female parental investment is even greater than in other species.[18] Should a woman have any one of her comparatively few eggs fertilized, she will normally be tied to the child's gestation for nine months and to its rearing for years. She therefore has good reason to be extremely selective about whose sperm she lets near her eggs. She need not think of it in these terms, of course: nature has built in emotions to guide her, like a wary desire for evidence of reliable and exclusive commitment on a suitor's part. If she seeks a long-term partner, she will wish to be especially chary, and a man strongly attracted to a particular woman therefore has strong incentives to try to overcome that chariness. As Seabright notes, "It's a spiral: the selectivity of the women encourages the persistence of men, and the more persistent are the men, the more selective the women have to be."[19]

That biological logic underlies the sonnet sequence, *Rime sparse* or *Canzoniere*, that Petrarch labored over from the 1320s to the 1370s: that, and its local cultural elaboration in the particularly high Christian valuation of female chastity. The combination allowed Petrarch's Laura to be valued not only for her unparalleled beauty but also for her resistance, her selectivity, her unparalleled virtue, even while Petrarch demonstrated his exceptional persistence, through all those sonnets, as if in proof of his incomparable commitment.

As soap operas, gossip columns, and political scandals attest, we remain perennially fascinated by who gets to partner whom. Romance seizes our attention in life and in story. After a wide cross-cultural search Patrick Colm Hogan notes that romances, stories ending in love, are the most pervasive form of narrative across all societies, much more widespread than tragedies.[20] The sonnet sequence as initiated by Petrarch consists of lyrics, of poems usually *without* stories, that can hold reader attention for long stretches through appealing to our fascination with the love-chase and through expressing male persistence with all the eloquence of the lyric poet.

We can understand the appeal the sonnet sequence had to poets in terms of artistic problems and solutions. As I have argued, our minds have evolved to be captured by story, and to read information as narrative if we possibly can.[21] Poets wanting to write longer poems almost invariably resort to narrative to hold attention. Lyrics of course can also engage our attention, and with special intensity, but they cannot easily sustain it long-term without resorting to the appeal of narrative and therefore ceasing to be lyrics. This poses a problem for the ambitious lyric poet. Sheer scale matters in art: great epics weigh more than great lyrics not just in pages but in artistic value. Individual Pushkin lyrics may be glorious, even perfect, but *Eugene Onegin*—a novel in fourteen-line stanzas like complexified sonnets—will always rate as his masterpiece. Lyric collections rarely become much more than the mere sum of their disparate parts, or even the sum of their summits. But by appealing to something so humanly central as the logic of sexual difference in love Petrarch could sustain an almost purely lyric sequence over, in his case, hundreds of poems. As I noted earlier, too, narrative earns attention by focusing on conflicts of wills. The Petrarchan sonnet sequence focuses on a conflict of will central to our nature, even if the resistance of the beloved remains only implicit in the eloquent persistence of the loving poet, and tends to stop narrative movement.

In culture as in nature it makes sense to build on preexisting solutions. Others adopted Petrarch's model, and nowhere more enthusiastically than in England in the 1580s and 1590s. But solutions also tend to entail their own problems. While the sonnet sequence reflects the logic of sexual difference, and so appeals to our fascination with romantic choice, it also protracts the sexual standoff between resistant female and persistent male poet to the point of sexual stalemate. As a genre, the sonnet sequence therefore chafes under its constraints. It has to appeal by varying the rhetoric of panegyric—the Poet's expressing his love for the beloved's unrivaled merits, as proof of his unmatched persistence and commitment—and by whatever psychological complexity can be wrung from the Poet's being torn between adoration and frustration. Sir Philip Sidney, in the most successful of English sonnet sequences before Shakespeare's, *Astrophil and Stella* (written in the 1580s, published posthumously in 1591), wittily encapsulates the combination (Sonnet 71):

> So while thy beauty draws the heart to love,
> As fast thy virtue bends that love to good.
> But ah, desire still cries, "Give me some food."

Even Sidney shows his awareness, from his opening sonnet, of the force of convention:

Loving in truth, and fain in verse my love to show,
That she (dear she) might take some pleasure of my pain;
Pleasure might cause her read, reading might make her know;
Knowledge might pity win, and pity grace obtain;
I sought fit words to paint the blackest face of woe,
Studying inventions fine, her wits to entertain;
Oft turning others' leaves, to see if thence would flow
Some fresh and fruitful showers upon my sun-burnt brain.
But words came halting forth, wanting invention's stay,
Invention, nature's child, fled step-dame study's blows,
And others' feet still seemed but strangers in my way.
Thus great with child to speak, and helpless in my throes,
    Biting my truant pen, beating myself for spite,
    "Fool," said my muse to me; "look in thy heart, and write."

And even Sidney, despite his Muse's advice, can often make only minor if graceful new shuffles while shackled by sonnet-sequence conventions.

The Mistress Sonnets

As his sonnet for Anne Hathaway suggests, Shakespeare had unusual gifts of language at eighteen, but he developed them far further to earn not just Anne, or even a coat of arms and a partnership in the King's Men, but the status of leading poet and playwright of his day or any other. When the plague closed the London theaters from 1592 until mid-1594, Shakespeare turned from plays to the narrative poems *Venus and Adonis* (1593) and *The Rape of Lucrece* (1594). These were wildly successful, the former running to at least sixteen editions by 1640. By the late 1590s, still in his early thirties, Shakespeare would be recognized as a modern classic in both verse and drama: Francis Meres in 1598 could write that "the sweet witty soul of Ovid lives in mellifluous and honey-tongued Shakespeare, witness his Venus and Adonis, his Lucrece. . . . As Plautus and Seneca are accounted the best for Comedy and Tragedy among the Latins, so Shakespeare among the English is the most excellent in both kinds for the stage."[22]

No wonder that by late in the first half-decade of his professional career this ambitious poet, having proved himself in drama—in comedy, tragedy and history—and in narrative verse—comic and tragic—turned to a new challenge, to lyric verse, in its currently most hotly contested form, the sonnet sequence, just at the peak of its popularity in the years 1592–95. Although he would not publish his *Sonnets* until 1609, internal evidence analyzed by Jackson and others shows that Shakespeare began writing them probably in 1594–95 and that, apart from Sonnet 145, the earliest group of sonnets composed were those numbered in the 1609 edition 127 to 152, the sonnets to a Mistress.[23]

(The internal evidence depends on the fact that, as Jackson notes, "every item of Shakespeare's lifetime word store was not equally accessible to him at any given moment."[24] Words Shakespeare rarely used tend to recur in works of similar date. By comparing the frequency with which the rare words in the sonnets recur in the plays, whose dates or order we *do* know, Jackson and others have been able to establish the strong links between the Mistress sonnets and the vocabulary of plays about 1594–95. Other kinds of internal evidence, such as rhyme, also converge on the conclusion that these sonnets are "the most homogeneously early of all," although they may well have been revised or added to.)[25]

Apart from Sonnet 145, we do not know in what order Shakespeare wrote the Mistress sonnets, but let's consider the one he (as it proves to have been)[26] placed first, 127:

In the old age black was not counted fair,
Or if it were it bore not beauty's name;
But now is black beauty's successive heir,
And beauty slandered with a bastard shame:
For since each hand hath put on Nature's power,
Fairing the foul with Art's false borrowed face,
Sweet beauty hath no name, no holy bower,
But is profaned, if not lives in disgrace.
Therefore my mistress' eyes are raven black,
Her eyes so suited, and they mourners seem
At such who, not born fair, no beauty lack,
Sland'ring creation with a false esteem:
    Yet so they mourn, becoming of their woe,
    That every tongue says beauty should look so.

In writing a sonnet sequence, Shakespeare follows the path of Petrarch and his English followers: he will make central the Poet's love for his fair mistress. Except that his mistress is not fair, but black. Precisely because of its centrality in literature, love as a theme risks the danger of repetition, and the loss of interest, the enfeeblement of attention, that results from habituation. Vladimir Nabokov, whom Edmund White rated the most romantic writer of the twentieth century, seized on our readiness for love stories, but removed the risk of satiation, by making his two central stories of insatiable love, *Lolita* and *Ada,* about an older man's desire for a twelve-year-old girl, and about a brother and sister passionately in love for a lifetime. Shakespeare, too, signals from the first that he will challenge expectation.

Here in the first of the Mistress sonnets he introduces right in the first line the traditional designation of black as "not counted fair," not beautiful, and through the first quatrain as a whole announces the paradox that black has now succeeded to the title of beauty, while beauty has been maligned as false. The second quatrain maintains the impersonal tone as it explains *why* beauty has lost its reputation, through its critique (ironically, despite the impersonality so far, a theme very personal to Shakespeare) of the art, or the falsehood, of makeup.[27] But it does nothing to show why old claims to be fair have proven false or drab beside the new claimant to be "beauty's successive heir." Then comes the *volta:* the Poet explains, by introducing his Mistress and her coloration—"Therefore my mistress' eyes are raven black"—and the fancy that her black colors could be mourning for those who adulterate the notion and truth of beauty through cosmetics.[28] The couplet clinches the case: her "mourning" colors, her unfeigned black, look so becoming "That every tongue says beauty should look so."

Coming, in the 1609 order, after 126 sonnets to or about a Fair Youth (of which more in Chapter 5), this sonnet switches explicitly to the poet's Mistress. She defies conventional standards of beauty in a way that seems to maximize beauty's truth and to reproach the current standards of would-be beauty, falsely beautified beauty. The poem indeed beautifully challenges conventions of praise and dispraise ("In the old age black was not counted fair"), but only as if to imply that the Mistress evades all dispraise and all reproach of false beauty. Had it come at the very beginning of the kind of sonnet sequence Shakespeare seems to have first had in mind, it would have easily refreshed the palate of readers sated by too many sugared sonnets.

Already at perhaps a mere eighteen Shakespeare had shown his feeling for form in the Anne Hathaway sonnet. Here, a decade or so later, his feeling for form and pattern have become much richer. Each line, each pair of lines, each quatrain forms its own unit, with a lucid logical flow from the name of beauty to the false look of modern beauty to the black mourning of "my mistress" and the new standards of beauty it sets. The love of contrast animating Sonnet 145 finds far more luxuriant expression here: *in the old age-now* and *black-fair* at the start of quatrain 1; *Nature's-Art's, Fairing-foul,* and *holy-profaned* in quatrain 2; *black-fair* again in quatrain 3. *Beauty* occurs six times (four times in the octave, twice in the sestet), *black* and *fair* three times each (twice each in the octave, once each in the sestet), as if each claimed "beauty" turn and turn about. Patterns like "black . . . beauty" (1–2), "black beauty's" (3), "beauty . . . black" (6–8), "beauty lack" (11), "beauty . . . look" (14), or "power . . . borrowed . . . bower . . . brows" (6–8, 10),[29] and "bore not . . . mourners . . . not born . . . mourn" (2, 10–13) weave through the poem, as do words for parts of the body, *hand, face, eyes, brows, tongue.* Other words than *beauty, black, fair, mourn,* also pointedly recur: *false, name, slander.*

Shakespeare has constructed Sonnet 127 to open a sequence of poems about a mistress who will overturn Petrarchan conventions. Here as often, it pays not to read into individual sonnets what we think we now know about the sonnets as a sequence, but to try to reconstruct the experience Shakespeare might have imagined his contemporary readers would have. He plays with the conventions gently here, which does not mean he will not play with them brutally in other sonnets in the sequence. Here *other* women may be foul ("Fairing the foul"), but not his mistress.

As we discover when we read on, Shakespeare, with the ambition and inventiveness he shows elsewhere in his art, has rethought the conventions deeply. Instead of writing sonnets for a woman as fair, as unattainable, and as chaste as Petrarch's Laura and the beloveds of Petrarch's imitators, he introduces a mistress who is not fair—though she is beautiful, in at least some of the poems—but dark in coloration.[30] More strikingly she is not only not unattainable but has been attained by many: she is the "bay where all men ride," or not a patch of individual land that can be fenced in ("a several plot") but "the wide world's common place" (137.6, 9–10). She can be not only not fair, but foul, and un-fair. The recurrent *not fair, foul, false, name, slander* in the opening sonnet, pointedly *not* applied to her there, except for her dark pigmentation, sound themes that will soon be openly aimed at her.

But to introduce from the first the inaccurate and premature notion of the dissolute Dark Lady common to modern discussions of the sonnets destroys the poet's structural design. "Dark Lady" in any case is a misnomer, because Shakespeare never calls her "lady," and refers to her only once as "dark."[31] I had thought of calling her the Un-Fair Mistress, but although that captures Shakespeare's language and her role better than Dark Lady, it also contravenes the openness from sonnet to sonnet, the uncertainty of relationship between poem and poem, that the poet seems to strive for in his lyric sequence.

Lyrics as Problem and Solution

All readers alert to Petrarchan conventions have seen that Shakespeare overturns them in the Mistress sonnets. I have expressed the challenge to conventions in terms of Shakespeare's attempt to solve the problem of habituation, the attenuation of attention, in sonnet sequence. Securing and sustaining attention is a problem for all artists. But I want to suggest also that Shakespeare faced a unique problem situation, at this point in his career—and that we have much to gain by considering problem situations at this individual level.[32] Having already triumphed in dramatic and narrative verse, a poet of his ambition had good reason to show what he could do in the absence of stories, to find what problems he could pose himself, and what solutions he could find, in making the most of lyrics as solo pieces and ensembles.

Shakespeare does not forgo, in fact he capitalizes on, the immediacy of the poetic voice engaged intimately and passionately with another. Much more often, proportionately, than other sonnet-sequence poets, he addresses either the Mistress, here, or later (in composition though not reading order), even more often, the Fair Youth, rather than talking about them in the third person.[33] In the Mistress sonnets he creates so well the illusion of himself engaged with a real woman who arouses his mingled love and hate, his desire and disgust, that readers and scholars for two hundred years have searched for real-life models. Even a highly regarded poet of our time, happy to stress how poets feign, can become angry over what he considers the misogyny the Mistress unleashes in Shakespeare.[34]

In view of Shakespeare's high-handed transformations of his source stories even in his history plays,[35] and the compelling evidence that the Rival Poet(s) of the sonnets are a composite of George Chapman, Michael Drayton, Ben Jonson, and Christopher Marlowe,[36] we can have little confidence that much historical fact lies behind the image of the Mistress. Just as he radically refashioned events and sequences in order to suit the dramatic needs of his plays, so he has presumably reworked his own knowledge or experience of women into the sonnets addressed to or about this dark woman. He does not attempt to present a consistent portrait of her or a consistent set of relations with her. As we have seen, he even includes within the sub-sequence a sonnet about Anne Hathaway.

But despite creating, in general, an intense emotional engagement with a Mistress (and later with a Youth), Shakespeare does not tell a story. He maximizes the openness of lyric, its freedom from the linearity of story. He offers each new poem as an unpredictable challenge, not least in the unpredictability of its relation to the poems before and after. He exploits the tension between the autonomy of each sonnet and the variety of its potential relations to its neighbors—emotional, thematic, verbal, rhyming, imagistic, structural; continuation, contrast, echo, variation, reversal.

Until two narrative sonnets at the end of the whole sequence that provide a deliberate segue into the narrative poem, "A Lover's Complaint," that rounds out the volume (of this, more in Chapter 8), Shakespeare writes 152 sonnets without narrative. Although most other Petrarchan sonnet sequences are primarily lyric, they do not avoid narrative as Shakespeare does. Sidney's *Astrophil and Stella,* for instance, begins with mininarrative in Sonnet 1, and another in Sonnet 2:

> I saw, and liked; I liked, but loved not;
> I loved, but straight did not what love decreed.
> At length to love's decrees I, forced, agreed.

Shakespeare chose another way.

Consider how he follows on from the first of the Mistress sonnets. Sonnet 127 itself, unlike Sidney's Sonnet 2, gives no indication of the inception, duration, or state of the Poet's relationship with his Mistress, although "Therefore my mistress' eyes . . ." (127.9) may suggest confident possession. The sonnet is in the third person, a declaration to all, proclaiming the Mistress's un-fairness as the epitome of truth and beauty in a modern world where beauty can be artificially applied. Such a sonnet could have opened a sequence that would refresh Petrarchan convention not by besmirching the Mistress but by proclaiming her unconventional integrity against the falsity of other women.

Sonnet 128, "How oft, when thou, my music, music play'st," switches from public proclamation to intimacy, to the second person, to playfulness and slightness, as the Poet stands by his Mistress playing the virginal and envies the keys meeting her fingers:

How oft . . .
Do I envy those jacks . . .

. . . .

Whilst my poor lips, which should that harvest reap,
At the wood's boldness by thee blushing stand.

He concludes by asking her to give the "saucy jacks" of the virginal "thy fingers, me thy lips to kiss." If this were part of a story, we might wonder whether this is a plea from a Petrarchan lover who hasn't yet had access to her lips—after all, he stands by, envious—or whether that final request ("Give . . . me thy lips to kiss") suggests a confident command, perhaps simply a new stirring of desire from someone the Mistress has already entertained well. Focusing on the playful analogy, Shakespeare shows no concern to narrow the situational range.

This sonnet addresses a "thou," whom we presume to be the Mistress of Sonnet 127, although the idea of her un-fairness here plays no part whatever. Rather than rattling Petrarchan conventions, Sonnet 128 seems to play happily within them. Then the famous and infamous Sonnet 129 crashes in with full force: "Th' expense of spirit in a waste of shame / Is lust in action. . . ." Its panting urgency, all the way to postcoital recoil, its fierce re-creation of lust before and revulsion after, explode Petrarchan convention completely. This time, the sonnet remains technically impersonal, with neither the Poet in first person, nor the Mistress in second or third person, yet the rushing syntax and the intensity and frankness of the subject make it appear psychologically and experientially immediate for writer and reader. And its dangerous dark energy radiates out—perhaps contaminating even the sonnets before, and almost inevitably disturbing those still to come.

Another famous sonnet follows, 130, "My mistress' eyes are nothing like the sun." Here the Poet confidently mocks sonnet conventions at their tiredest, rejecting the falsity of habitual hyperbole but expressing a realistic esteem for his Mistress. As its presence in so many anthologies shows, the poem can stand perfectly on its own, but it also replays and modifies two themes from 127, the blackness of his mistress and, in a different way, the contrast between honest truth and conventional exaggerations of beauty, by women in 127, and by their Poet-Lovers here. The sonnet's quietly proud rejection of false enchantments links tantalizingly with the disenchantment of 129, but with none of its immediate predecessor's bitterness or its context of lust.

Sonnet 131 begins "Thou art as tyrannous, so as thou art, / As those whose beauties proudly make them cruel." Since the start of the Mistress poems we have had third person, second, neither, third, and now, again, second. Focusing on the same relationship, Shakespeare orients and engages us from sonnet to sonnet yet also keeps uncertain where we will stand and face next. When he calls the Mistress tyrannous, is she tyrannous like the mistresses of other sonnet sequences, resisting his love? Others may disparage her, he declares, but

> Thy black is fairest in my judgement's place.
>   In nothing art thou black save in thy deeds,
>   And thence this slander as I think proceeds.

Does he mean by her black deeds, her tyranny toward him? Or does he mean more, something rather more troubling, perhaps a reputation for the "lust in action" of Sonnet 129? "Now," the Poet had declared in Sonnet 127, "is black beauty's successive heir, / And beauty slandered with a bastard shame." There, his Mistress, though not "fair," had been the modern epitome of beauty and truth, in opposition to those "who, not born fair, no beauty lack, / Sland'ring creation with a false esteem." Now *she* is slandered (131.14), although the Poet still proclaims her black fairest for him, in line 12. But then comes the couplet. Stephen Booth captures one possible nuance of the couplet, if we read it, as we may well, in the darkest light. Commenting on "I think" in line 14, Booth finely glosses: "I believe, I venture to say (the tone of modest, responsible, respectful diffidence that the speaker affects by this phrase is so at odds with the substance of the charge casually levelled in line 13 that it transforms the whole couplet into a single graceful razor stroke—one that is especially damaging because the speaker's tone assumes that his victim's values are the ones on which his supposedly comforting explanation rests and that she hasn't the moral sensitivity to notice that she has been cut apart)."[37]

Yet Sonnet 132 returns to what seems much more innocent play with black and beauty, reminiscent of 127. Sonnet 127's image of the Mistress's black as mourning returns, but in a quite different manner. Rather than her black being mourning for the falsehood of artificial beauty aids, the Poet now asks her heart "To mourn for me, . . . And suit thy pity like in every part" (compare "Her brows so *suited,* and they *mourners* seem," 127.10). The verbal and imagistic echo of 127 comes with a change in emotional key, as here the Poet implores the Mistress whose heart "torment[s] me with disdain" to pity him—presumably to grant him his desire, like the standard plea of the standard Poet-Lover; or is this somehow an echo of a completely different kind of pity, in connection with the black deeds of Sonnet 131? Emphasizing her black beauty, the Poet here makes a comparison—

And truly not the morning sun of heaven
Better becomes the grey cheeks of the east,
Nor that full star that ushers in the even
Doth half that glory to the sober west
As those two mourning eyes become thy face

—that accords oddly with the rejection of panegyric comparison in "My mistress' eyes are nothing like the sun" (130.1), while the "*mourning* eyes [which] *become* thy face" chime in a quite different way with 127.13's description of her eyes: "Yet so they *mourn, becoming* of their woe."

If Shakespeare has sought to make a narrative of these sonnets, he would be performing disastrously. Instead, he seems to have other aims. He makes the most of love as a subject, and of the Poet's voice, and of the sense of dramatic intimacy and emotional intensity between real individuals that the love lyric at its best can provide, but he probes what he can do not *with* story but in the absence of story. In narrative, the patterns of plot, of goal, action, reaction, and outcome, can direct and consume the reader's attention and constrain the writer's imaginative freedom. Without the domination of sequence and causality, Shakespeare here opens up new spaces for play with pattern, within the sonnet, in its relation to other sonnets around it, and in its relation to the sonnet sequence as a form.

Rather than trying to read the sonnets as a narrative, as a kind of verse journal, I suggest we should see Shakespeare's art here as in some ways like a kaleidoscope—a device that would not be invented for another two centuries. A kaleidoscope continually taps or shakes its colored chips into new configurations, often strangely similar from tap to tap, yet with eye- and mind-teasing similarities to recent configurations, or perhaps, after a more vigorous shake, suddenly quite different, yet even then within a recognizable range of combinatorial possibilities defined by the free elements and the fixed mirrors, Shakespeare inserts as it were into his kaleidoscope two key character chips, Poet and Mistress; a range of emotional and mood chips; a handful of core thematic chips, love, hate, truth, falsehood, beauty, ugliness, desire, disgust; and terms and images, echoes and contrasts within these sonnets and from other sonnet sequences, like *fair, black, dark, foul, eyes, hearts, blind, see;* more chips for tone and voice—then encases them all within the sonnet form, the angled mirrors within his kaleidoscope tube.

Unlike a story, the sonnets have no firm progression and no privileged final state, but may offer fresh configurations at each new tap or shake as Shakespeare shakes up the all-too-static situation of persistent Poet and resistant Mistress that structures most sonnet sequences. He introduces a situation less than clear or consistent, full of passion but also, increasingly, of a corrosive uncertainty or open distaste that still does not dispel desire.

Precisely because they lack the fixed order of story, his sonnets can recombine more or less pure patterns of verbal form and the intensely human patterns of character, situation, emotion, and theme. In the mostly later-composed but earlier-placed sonnets to the Youth, Shakespeare will add a much wider emotional and thematic range. But even here he can freshen and deepen the psychology of love, less by maintaining and developing a consistent characterization of the Mistress and a consistent development of his relationship with her than by jiggling the kaleidoscope in new ways to examine possibilities from different sides. What would it mean to see the woman you love unvalued, disparaged, even despised by others? To believe her virtuous and discover her foul?

To be besotted and obsessed yet to know her infidelity? To have her resist you while she accepts others? To have her even steal your best friend? To hate yourself for loving? To saturate yourselves in deception and self-deception? To experience the cruelty not of the chastity of the conventional Petrarchan mistress, but of promiscuity—a cruelty augmented at times by her inaccessibility to you? Even to joke obsessively about her promiscuity and her unavailability?

These are exactly the kinds of compromised feelings that Shakespeare could not explore readily on stage—at least until *Antony and Cleopatra*. Despite his love of bawdy, too, some personal sense of public decorum seems to make his plays more sexually conservative than those of other dramatists of his time,[38] and to limit the exploration of the darker dilemmas of desire he can treat here. The kaleidoscopic structure of the sonnets allows for the recurrent eddying, the surge and backwash and vortices of emotions and relationships not readily explored in the more linear course of the stories that he could offer his theatrical audience. The Mistress sonnets do follow a general trend from positive and desiring to negative and recoiling—we do need to believe that at some stage, as in 127, the Poet has reason to want her as his Mistress—but that trend can be disrupted by local unpredictability and never implies a definite sequence of events. The last of the poems addressed to the Mistress, 152, returns to the "fair-foul" opposition of the first Mistress poem in a much more dismissive key: "For I have sworn thee fair: more perjured eye, / To swear against the truth so foul a lie." But even this final poem begins "In loving thee thou know'st I am forsworn." The Mistress sonnets end resoundingly but without finality: the love continues, however tainted.

Solution as New Problem

Despite the opportunities Shakespeare at thirty or so could find in the Mistress sonnets, their very logic could not sustain a sequence. Entering the most competitive of literary arenas in the first half of the 1590s, the poet could hope to earn attention by overturning the core convention of sonnet sequence, the assumption of male persistence and female resistance. But this bold move could not lead to a publishable countersequence. Indeed, Shakespeare's very challenge to expectations by focusing on a woman who does not need persistent pursuit by the male, and who even solicits unresistant males, means that although these poems can surprise and amuse, especially in a line like "the bay where all men ride," the sequence undermines its own rationale. If the Mistress mostly does not resist the Poet or others, and does not hold his affection, even if she still stirs his desire, the basis for the persistence that sustains older sonnet sequences soon falls away.

For the most part these sonnets on a Mistress track the disenchantments of avid and deceitful desire, and although their tones and strategies can change from poem to poem, many readers, myself included, also find them en masse often thin and sour. Wordsworth called them "abominably harsh, obscure, and worthless," and in our own day Paterson can refer to "the toxic Dark Lady junk."[39] A sonnet sequence inverting Petrarchan conventions through a Mistress in multiple ways "not fair" could not yield a whole ironic series. Shakespeare would publish the Mistress poems only fifteen years or so after beginning them, and only after he had added many more sonnets to an even more attention-catching and much less self-defeating sub-sequence.

The limited success of the Mistress poems accords with Darwinian explanations of genius: with no possibility of a prompt from some higher intelligence already in possession of answers, even genius will tend to produce a wide range of greater and lesser successes or comparative failures.[40] Since real creativity requires exploration through the vastness of possibility space, there can be no sure routes to success. But one imperfect solution may provide the elements and the impetus for much richer success.

5

Love and Time

The Youth

Upsetting Petrarch

The best evidence currently available suggests that Shakespeare wrote most of the first 126 sonnets later in the 1590s than the Mistress poems, and that he wrote those in the last part of this section, from about Sonnets 104 to 126, in the 1600s.[1] If the 1609 volume's order was the author's, as now seems to have been demonstrated beyond reasonable doubt,[2] he poses in Sonnets 1 to 126 a much more surprising and fertile challenge to Petrarch than in the Mistress sonnets that begin with 127.

We have more information about the sonnets than was available sixty years ago, more even than twenty or fifteen years ago, and it seems wrong not to avail ourselves of it. Nevertheless if we assume, as this information suggests, that Shakespeare himself arranged *Shake-speares Sonnets,* we can also try to bring to bear only the information the poet thought would be available to informed readers of his time when they opened the volume: information, that is, especially about the tradition of sonnets and of sonnet sequences, and about English language and society current in 1609, but not information about the as-yet-unread "ensuing sonnets." However much they may keep an eye on posterity, poets know they have to work almost immediately on their immediate audience.

Sonnet 1

Reading Sonnet 1 as a reader of 1609 might first do, therefore, we have to set aside notions that this is the first of a sequence of sonnets addressed to a Fair Youth, let alone conjectures about who such a youth might be, and just read:

> From fairest creatures we desire increase,
> That thereby beauty's rose might never die,
> But as the riper should by time decease,
> His tender heir might bear his memory:
> But thou, contracted to thine own bright eyes,
> Feed'st thy light's flame with self-substantial fuel,
> Making a famine where abundance lies,
> Thy self thy foe, to thy sweet self too cruel:
> Thou that art now the world's fresh ornament,
> And only herald to the gaudy spring,
> Within thine own bud buriest thy content,
> And, tender churl, mak'st waste in niggarding:
>> Pity the world, or else this glutton be,
>> To eat the world's due, by the grave and thee.

Reading lyric poetry, we expect not a story to focus our attention—a relevance supplied by characters and their aims in an unfolding narrative context—but an implicit invitation to other kinds of relevance, relevance to ourselves, to us all, to life as we know or can imagine it. Lyric poems invite us to a game of skill, sometimes easy, sometimes tricky, that we can enjoy best when we let words and patterns, however general or particular, however familiar or novel, resonate to the utmost. Readers of Elizabethan sonnet sequences expected to enjoy the sonnet game, well played, to be privy to appeals from persistent poets to resistant beloveds, and to find resonance in the urgency, the eloquence, and the emotional complexity of love.

Shakespeare's Sonnet 1 opens with an inclusive generalization, making explicit its relevance to all: "From fairest creatures we desire increase." Oddly, the poet takes a psychological truism—"We desire the fairest creatures"—and turns it into a general, somewhat implausibly disinterested, claim about our responses to beauty. Foregrounding the beauty so important in the sonnet tradition, the sonnet expands on the idea through the first quatrain: ". . . That thereby beauty's rose might never die." Shakespeare draws here on a commonplace—and therefore an easy—image, but his fresh formulation stipulates not just a rose, but "beauty's rose," the rose itself as the concrete emblem and epitome of natural beauty, and therefore, in this locution, the perfection of beauty, "beauty's most beautiful," but also, with its short-lived blossoms, an emblem of the fleeting frailty of beauty.

Beauty reproduces itself to persist, through regeneration, beyond death. That general rule fills the first quatrain, but the second turns from the general to the particular, and from the rule to the exception: "*But* thou . . ." Neither Shakespeare nor the title of his volume—unlike his contemporaries' sonnet sequences from

Aurora to *Zepheria*—offers any indication who "thou" might be, but the imagery increases in intensity and reproach: "thou, contracted to thine own bright eyes," shrunk down (contracted) to your own self-adoring eyes, betrothed (contracted, in another sense) only to yourself. The images tumble over one another: the candle burning itself in self-regard ("Feed'st thy light's flame with self-substantial fuel"); famine; enmity; cruelty.

The third quatrain starts again with the emphatic "Thou," still an exception to the first quatrain's general rule. Its first two lines offer a compliment—"Thou that art now the world's fresh ornament, / And only herald to the gaudy spring"—that will only add to the charge when the attack resumes, with another reproachful pun: "Within thine own bud buriest thy content": you bury all you might contain ("thy content") within your young self; you feel happiness ("thy content") only at your pleasure in yourself.

The couplet closes and intensifies the sonnet with an imploring imperative, "Pity the world," and the repellent rebuke, with its extraordinary imagery of autophagy and infantivorism, "or else this glutton be / To eat the world's due, by the grave and thee."

The whole poem is strange, and strangely intense, in any number of ways. It has the argument for procreation that could be expected in a male-to-female seduction poem. Indeed, a first-time reader, knowing that the poet is male, and that sonnets are usually addressed to beloveds, would assume that Shakespeare addresses a woman—especially as he implicitly classes the addressee as one of the "fairest creatures"—until the oxymoronic "tender churl" of line 12 indicates that "thou" must be male. ("His" in Elizabethan usage often meant *its,* as it does in line 4, referring presumably to "the riper" or to "beauty's rose.")[3]

Both before the surprise of line 12, for readers expecting a love poem to a woman, and after, once we recognize it as addressed to a man, Sonnet 1 seems decidedly odd. Sonnets as seduction poems may vouch for the poets' love, as a way to eventually winning the women's requital of their love, but Shakespeare's first sonnet exhorts "thou" to reproduce without mentioning either the poet or his love for the addressee.

Evolutionary biologists recognize reproduction and survival as the fundamental goals of all organisms. In ordinary human terms we naturally speak, instead, of love and death, key concerns of life as of literature. Here in Sonnet 1, the poet urges "thou" to reproduce "thy self" because death inevitably waits. We could see a strict evolutionary logic here, in thoroughly non-Shakespearean terms: all organisms, however long-lived, suffer environmental or internal insults, like fire, drought, radiation damage, attack by other organisms, wear and tear, or disease. Life could not succeed by creating eternal organisms, since none could last forever. But if an organism's genes can reproduce, starting over in a fresh cellular package in the next generation, free of any accumulated damage, the instructions for that organism can in a sense circumvent death by passing on undamaged genes, which in turn can be passed on to subsequent generations.

Of course that is not what motivates us to reproduce. Nature has built urgent desire into sexually reproducing organisms in order to entice us into coupling with partners whose genes our offspring can share. Nature would have quickly reached a dead end had it relied on persuading organisms to reproduce in order to stave off eventual accumulated damage, and therefore death: a rather forbidding, almost paralyzing, kind of instruction. Yet that, without the language of the modern biologist, is exactly what Shakespeare seems to urge the "thou" of Sonnet 1 to do. Reproduce, or consume yourself in death.

Other modern biological terms accentuate the strangeness of the sonnet. Nature guides us through what biologists call proximate mechanisms (in this case, sexual desire as motivation) to serve ultimate functions (in this case, reproduction). We need not know anything about the reasons for a proximate mechanism such as fear, hunger, or desire in order for it to serve its ultimate biological end of enhancing our survival, in the first two cases, or our reproduction, in the third. We simply respond to its promptings: we flee, we eat, or we mate. Yet Shakespeare urges "thou" to act not on the prompt of immediate motivation, desire, but for the sake of ultimate function, reproduction.

Did he not understand human motivation? Hardly—indeed, has anyone understood it better? And as the quotations from his plays in the previous chapter attest, he understands the equation of sonnets with attempted seduction. He also recognizes the pattern of male persistence in the face of female resistance that characterizes sonnet sequences. In Sonnet 1 he even uses key words from the Petrarchan tradition, *cruel* and *pity,* but not in the usual Petrarchan sense, "cruel to me" in not returning my love, and "pity me," so committed to love for thee, by returning my love. Instead, his "thou" is "to thy sweet self too cruel" in not having children, and should "pity the world," by producing copies of "thy sweet self."

Sonnet 1 addresses large issues, of relevance to all readers, indeed to all life, but in a way almost demotivating, despite its personal and urgent tone. Shakespeare here makes the most of the lack of defined situation that the brevity of lyric verse enables. What makes his relation to "thou" so urgent? We simply do not know. Readers of the sonnets in 1609, like modern readers used to lyrics, would have been struck by the absence of any reference to the poet. The poets of late Elizabethan sonnet sequences introduce themselves early and emphatically. Sidney opens the first sonnet of *Astrophil and Stella,* "Loving in truth, and fain in verse *my* love to show." *I, me, my,* and *myself* occur ten times in his opening sonnet, whose last line discloses another equivalent, in the *thy* addressed to the speaker: "'Fool,' said my muse to me; 'look in thy heart, and write.'" The first sonnet in Samuel Daniel's *Delia* (1592) has fourteen *I*'s or *my*'s. The first in Michael Drayton's *Idea's Mirror* (1594 and later revisions) has four pronouns referring directly to the poet, and nine *he*'s or *his*, all part of an extended simile that ultimately refers to the poet. The opening sonnet in Edmund Spenser's *Amoretti* (1595) includes five *I*'s or *my*'s, and in Richard Barnfield's *Cynthia* (1595), six. Shakespeare, by contrast, to look a little ahead, includes no reference to himself, no *I, me,* or *my*, until Sonnet 10.

And if sonnets reflect the logic of male competition in sexual selection, the last thing we might expect would be one male exhorting another—and therefore a potential rival—to procreate, with no matter *which* woman.

Shakespeare's time may have seen sonnets as the quintessence of love poetry, but although he, too, has made brilliant capital out of the same supposition, most memorably in *Romeo and Juliet,* he begins his sonnet sequence urging someone to procreate, in a manner as remote as possible from love: he exhorts another to reproduce in order to elude the total encroachment of death. Deeply odd and original as the first sonnet in a sequence, Sonnet 1 challenged expectations in 1609, and still challenges them, in ways much more complex than the far shallower reversals, *fair* versus *dark, black, unfair* or *foul,* in the earlier Mistress poems.

Yet, at the same time, Shakespeare ties this sonnet closely to the opening of the Mistress sonnets and in doing so follows and deliberately highlights the two-part structure common in other English sonnet sequences, ultimately reflecting the two-part structure of Petrarch's sequence, before and after Laura's death.[4] Both Shakespeare's Sonnet 1 and Sonnet 127 have *fair* in line 1, *beauty's* in line 2,[5] and *heir* and either *bear* (indicative) or *bore* (subjunctive) also within the first quatrain. The fresh quatrain that first introduces "thou" in Sonnet 1 and "my mistress" in Sonnet 127 begins with a line contrasting their eyes: "But thou, contracted to thine own bright eyes" and "Therefore my mistress' eyes are raven black." The next line in Sonnet 1, line 6, and the same line in Sonnet 127, are saturated with alliterations on *f* and consonance on *l* ("*F*eed'st thy *l*ight's *f*lame with se*lf*-substantia*l f*ue*l*"; "*F*airing the *f*ou*l* with Art's *f*a*l*se borrowed *f*ace"), and in the next two lines, *sweet* occurs in both sonnets.[6] In both, the sestets feature funeral imagery in both quatrain and couplet ("buriest thy content . . . by the grave and thee"; "they mourner seem . . . so they mourn"). Shakespeare subtly mines the conventions—here, the two-part structure of sonnet sequences—even as he also subtly undermines them. Or, in my terms: he ramps up cognitive play with pattern (and decidedly *nonnarrative* pattern at that), a pattern carefully enough hidden, albeit in plain view, not to be detected for four centuries.

Sonnets and Strategies

Not just the first but the first seventeen sonnets exhort "thou" to have children, and with much the same intensity as Sonnet 1.[7] Not only Sonnet 1 but all seventeen sonnets in this sub-sequence surprise by their intensity and their intimate exhortation to an unknown addressee to pass on his beauty to a new generation. What are we to make of this extraordinary insistence?

We do not know the man the poet addresses, or his relationship to the Poet, who does not even introduce himself until well into the sub-sequence, or why the Poet feels he has the right to reproach this person so familiarly and forthrightly, or why he utters the same reproach so repeatedly, or to what extent he writes on behalf of himself, or particular others, or all offended by the addressee's failure to put his beauty to use.

Sonnet sequences traditionally focus on the love a poet feels for a beloved woman he addresses and adores and implores. Why does this long sub-sequence of exhortations to a Young Man to breed open Shakespeare's sonnets, and how does it lead into the sonnets that follow?

Especially when we face such a nonobvious strategy, we can seek to understand a writer's aims by attempting to reconstruct his or her problem situation. As I suggested in the previous chapter, focusing on the evidence of the first Mistress sonnets, Shakespeare, already highly successful as a writer of plays and narrative poems, appears to have set himself as a problem to make the most of the preeminent form of lyric in his time, sonnets in sequence, and to make the most of the differences between the possibilities of both drama and narrative and those to be found in lyric verse.

At the level of the individual sonnet, he maximizes the opportunities of the single line, the sonnet's structure, its patterns, and its invitation to immediate rereading. At the level of the sequence, he exploits the absence of an explicit situation and a clearly developing story, but still avails himself of love as the established theme of sonnet sequences and as a theme of intense appeal to all. Yet to avoid the habituation, the flagging of interest through repetition, of still another sequence to a supremely fair but firmly resistant beloved, he first seeks to seize the attention of readers by writing poems to a Mistress who is not fair or resistant and who, indeed, far from resisting males, persistently invites them with her wicked glances as well her good looks.

The harshness and the ironic detachment of the Mistress poems offered a radical, eye-catching reversal of sonnet-sequence conventions, but they also proved to be emotionally thin soil, not sufficient in themselves for a whole sequence. At some point near the mid-1590s,[8] Shakespeare found another way to take the expectations of sonnet readers by surprise, another way to earn, and this time to hold, their attention, by challenging, from an even more unexpected direction, the sonnet-sequence norm of male persistence and female resistance. What if he were to introduce not a female beauty, unfair and foul and all too attainable, but a male beauty, fair but resisting all, and indeed, in contrast to the Mistress, fair in all senses?

Even the greatest writers seek to reduce their invention costs while still availing themselves of the benefits of novelty. Recombination of successful existing design offers one of the likeliest routes to creativity in biological evolution as in human invention. Shakespeare had written two highly successful narrative poems about exceptional beauties who aroused desire in others but resisted even the most persistent of suitors. In *Venus and Adonis* (1593), a young male's extraordinary beauty fires the ardor of the goddess of love. Adonis' amusingly adamant resistance provokes Venus' unrelenting persistence, in arguments not unlike those of Shakespeare's Sonnets 1–17:

> Things growing to themselves are growth's abuse;
> Seeds spring from seeds, and beauty breedeth beauty:
> Thou wast begot: to get it is thy duty.
> Upon the earth's increase why shouldst thou feed,
> Unless the earth with thy increase be fed?
> By law of nature thou art bound to breed,
> That thine may live, when thou thyself art dead:
>> And so in spite of death thou dost survive,
>> In that thy likeness still is left alive. (166–174)

In the tragic companion piece to *Venus and Adonis*, *The Rape of Lucrece* (1594), female beauty inspires brutal male persistence despite unyielding female resistance.

Shakespeare begins in Sonnets 1–17 not with a resisting female but with a resisting *male*, creating his new ploy both by inverting the premise of his Mistress sonnets, where the female resists no one, and by drawing on the success and the surprise of male resistance in his *Venus and Adonis*. By introducing a male as heart-turningly fair as Adonis, Shakespeare can keep the focus on beauty so central to sonnet sequences in a way quite the converse of the non-fair but darkly beautiful Mistress. And he can generate in his own voice the pressure of persuasion he gives to Venus and Tarquin, as if the exhortation of the Fair Youth to breed is a matter of life and death for him.

But he can also make the most of the contrast between narrative and lyric. In both *Venus and Adonis* and *The Rape of Lucrece* Shakespeare sets the scene quickly and moves swiftly to a sharply defined conflict of wills. Desire drives Venus and Tarquin to their arguments as seducers, and desperate resistance drives Adonis and Lucrece to their rebuttals. But much of the strange magic of Shakespeare's first seventeen sonnets comes from the absence of a defined situation and a defined relationship, and from the contrast between the presence and persistence of the Poet and the absence of the Fair Youth and the silence of his resistance.

Venus and Tarquin address their objects of desire face to face, in urgent speech, even if they happen to speak in Shakespeare's shapely stanzas, and Adonis and Lucrece reply with equal urgency. In his first seventeen sonnets Shakespeare does not speak to someone present but *writes* to someone absent, and as a Poet, with the time and the experience to compose himself:

Who will believe my verse in time to come . . .
If I could write the beauty of your eyes . . .
    But were some child of yours alive that time,
    You should live twice, in it, and in my rhyme. (17)

The two contending character-pairs in the two narrative poems engage in urgent argument and counterargument, but Shakespeare as Poet in the sonnets can expatiate, can make the most of the other's silence, can rethink the theme at leisure from a different angle and fashion it into another carefully constructed sonnet, even as he moves on, toward the end of the sub-sequence, to stress that the Time that will "un-fair" the Fair Youth (5.4), and that he is therefore "all in war with" (15.13), can be resisted by the immortality of his verse.

Venus and Tarquin, like the poets of other sonnet sequences, persist against resistance, out of their own urgent personal desire. At the start of his own sonnets Shakespeare surprises by having no self-interested desire, as the Fair Youth displays no desire outside himself, in a world that the Poet nevertheless recognizes, in the first line of the first sonnet, but only impersonally, as driven by desire ("From fairest creatures we desire increase"). Yet he makes his argument as persistent and passionate as those of Venus and Tarquin, as if it were a matter of life and death, and as far from the disenchantment of most of the Mistress sonnets as can be. He turns his persistence into a series of virtuoso variations on this one theme, as if to demonstrate that, if the Fair Youth himself refuses to procreate, his beauty at least can inspire the Poet's imagination to go forth and multiply.

Poet and Fair Youth: Love

Shakespeare seems to have asked himself at some point not only, what if a male beauty resists all, despite attracting all, but what if the Poet becomes enamored of him? (The dates of probable composition suggest he could have taken his cue from the homoerotic sequence of twenty sonnets addressed to Ganymede in Richard Barnfield's *Cynthia*, 1595.) What if passionate concern turns into enchantment, into love? Or, at least, in the course of these first seventeen sonnets, Shakespeare lets it appear as if he begins to feel and express his love for the Young Man, whether he simply sees a new poetic possibility, or whether he responds to the beauty of a real young man, whom perhaps he has been commissioned to exhort to marriage.[9]

As we have seen, Shakespeare diverges from sonnet-sequence norms by not introducing himself until Sonnet 10. Pointedly, that introduction occurs in a sonnet whose first quatrain ends "Grant, if thou wilt, thou art beloved of many, / But that thou none lov'st is most evident," and ends with the first reference to the Poet's love for the Fair Youth: "Make thee another self for love of me, / That beauty still may live in thine or thee." Sonnet 13 raises the emotional heat:

> O that you were your self; but, love, you are
> No longer yours than you your self here live:
> Against this coming end you should prepare.
> .   .   .   .
>   . . . dear my love, you know
> You had a father, let your son say so.[10]

Shakespeare avoids story—the personal love of Poet and Youth enters as established fact, not as new development—but avails himself of the intensity of feeling and the intimacy of address that lyric allows. The emotion and its open resonance matter, not the circumstances of story, not a question like, when does his intense concern for the Fair Youth, or his admiration for his beauty, turn to love: before the first sonnet, or as he writes them?

Shakespeare has now awakened the emotional enchantment that he needs in order to deal with love with the intensity and mystery it deserves, and that the disenchantment of the Mistress sonnets rarely allowed. His new focus lets the Poet express love as an ideal—the theme at the center of the sonnet-sequence tradition—with a seemingly intensely personal, perhaps even transgressive, passion that makes it hard to see it as mere repetition of tired sonneteering conventions.

Immortality by Another Route

Even if the Young Man's beauty makes Shakespeare desire him, the Poet cannot be "sexually selected" by the Fair Youth, in the sense that they cannot produce children together. Of course they could engage in sex, but Sonnet 20, the most sexually explicit of the Fair Youth sonnets, rules this possibility out, whether this reflects biographical fact or only serves poetic fiction.[11] But by virtue of the Young Man's beauty inspiring him to write the poems that record the impact of his looks, Shakespeare can, within the fiction of the sonnets, produce images of the Young Man that offer him another way of cheating time, another road to immortality. He expresses a love that *he* as poet and as male can repay best by extolling and preserving the Young Man's image for the future, in the face of time and death, in the ensuing sonnets.

The theme of immortality through verse begins in Sonnet 15, the first sonnet that does *not* urge the Young Man to reproduce, and continues through three sonnets tightly linked in a thesis-antithesis-synthesis structure. In Sonnet 15, the Poet stresses his own role in "engraft[ing] you new" in his verse; in Sonnet 16, he suggests that "a mightier way" for the Fair Youth to resist time would be to father his own children; in Sonnet 17 he proposes *both* modes of living on: "But were some child of yours alive that

time, / You should live twice, in it, and in my rhyme." The next
Sonnet, 18, "Shall I compare thee to a summer's day?," marks a
shift in tone and direction, but it also acts as a clincher to the
three sonnets that precede, a declaration of a theme that will persist, and, in its own memorability, a confirmation of its closing
claim: "So long as men can breathe or eyes can see, / So long lives
this, and this gives life to thee."

The new countertheme to the theme of love allows Shakespeare to foreground the risk of death and extinction that love
drives us to overcome. Now he can not only dwell on the two
greatest themes in life and literature, love and death, or reproduction and survival—perhaps the only ones that, in the absence of
narrative, could sustain interest through quite so many variations. He can also foreground the role of art as offering another
way of circumventing death, the richest way, apart from producing offspring or from the consolations that religion proposes[12]—as
we will see in more detail in Chapter 7.

Variety

The Fair Youth, in marked contrast to the Mistress, is declared to
be fair in all senses: he combines "truth and beauty" (14), he is
"Fair, kind, and true" (105). But despite this ground rule, Shakespeare can make the ground shift as he turns love around from
every angle. After offering a range of variations on the single theme
of procreation in the first seventeen sonnets, like a series of gentle
taps on the kaleidoscope that reconfigures similar patterns each
time, Shakespeare now shakes things up, demonstrating in the
first sonnets that follow just how much bold variation of subject,
structure, and tone he can incorporate within the constant focus
on the Fair Youth.[13]

Like love itself, the premise of the Youth's resisting others and even the premise of his being fair in all senses need not always hold. He need not always resist all; he may even not resist the unresistant Mistress (see Sonnets 40–42 and 133–134). In a conventional sonnet sequence, the woman's accepting another suitor would be unthinkable: it would promptly end the poet's pursuit and the poems. Here, by contrast, the Mistress's infidelity is an ironic and comic given—although it also stops the rich elaboration of her sub-sequence—but the Young Man's infidelity, emotional or sexual, need not cause the Poet to break off: he does not have the reason for requiring proof of fidelity in the Young Man that a male seriously wooing a female might have.

The Fair Youth's friendship can become clouded even early in the sequence (33–34), and even at this stage the Poet's trust in him can be somehow deeply violated by the Youth's behavior:

. . . loathsome canker lives in sweetest bud.
All men make faults, and even I in this,
Authorizing thy trespass with compare. (35)

As Jackson observes, the Poet struggles to keep to his idealizing vision of the Young Man and their love[14]—despite not only the Youth's betrayals but even his own. Shakespeare's preference here for openness over linearity, for kaleidoscopic recombination over causality, for lyric over narrative sequence, allows him to explore in unpredictable ways love's pleasures and pains, its selflessness and selfishness, its constancy and its changeability, its security and insecurity, its mutuality and its occasional one-sidedness; love and sex, love and friendship; love and praise, love and blame; love and presence, love and absence; love as glory, love as shame; love and truth, love and deceit, love and self-deception.

Not only does the Fair Youth sub-sequence allow Shakespeare to explore so many sides of love—and immortality through *art* rather than through *nature's* way of transcending individual death, by reproduction; it also allows him to raise the questions of status he explores so often in his drama. Poets in conventional sonnet sequences kneel low before the pedestals on which they place their beloveds, in order to provide proof of their exceptional emotional commitment. Shakespeare, too, abases himself and exalts the young man, but the effect is decidedly less conventional. As we will see in Chapter 6, in the space between one male's self-abasement and his exaltation of another, Shakespeare can probe the role of social hierarchy and the relationship between poet and patron.

The Sonnets' Challenge: Lyric, Not Story

With the Fair Youth as a premise, Shakespeare now had the basis for a whole sonnet sequence, and in the two-part form common since Petrarch:[15] in Shakespeare's case, first the Fair Youth and then the Un-Fair Mistress. As a storyteller in drama and verse, Shakespeare knew both the impact of one-on-one intensity and the potential for one relationship to destabilize others. Here he makes the most of his near-minimal cast of three, with the emotional force-field of the Poet, the sole speaker, in uncertain relation to the emotional force-fields of the other two—silent—characters, themselves uncertain in relation to each other once the Youth proves, at some point, no longer resistant toward at least one woman, the Poet's own Mistress.

With a multitude of major themes at hand—love and friendship, death and time, art and status—Shakespeare as lyricist can keep the reader unsure from sonnet to sonnet just what will feature next, in a way that as storyteller, constrained by sequence and cause and effect, he could do much less easily. And instead of developing the sequentiality of a story, he makes the most of the kaleidoscope effect, shaking up the human elements in his sequence—Poet, Youth, and Mistress—in ways that also remain unpredictable from poem to poem. Each sonnet's situation can be a surprise, unrestricted by what has gone before—a sonnet declaring "But you like none, none you, for constant heart" (53.14) can follow poems that deplore the Youth's betrayal of the Poet—so that a lyric can resonate within its own solitary space or in more or less concord or contrast with its neighbors.

Shakespeare sets up the sonnets to exploit our strong default tendency to make sense of things in narrative terms if we possibly can. He offers us hints of strong narrative scenarios, like the Youth's succumbing to the temptations of the Mistress, or his being wooed by a Rival Poet or Poets. But at the same time he frustrates narrative in maintaining the interest of the openness of lyric situations, as when Sonnets 40–42 imply a sexual relationship between the Youth and the Poet's female love, not yet identified as the Mistress, while later poems return to a sense of unruffled emotional closeness of Poet and Youth, or to paeans to the emotional truth and fidelity of the Youth. Paterson, as I noted earlier, maintains, as if there were no other option, that "The Sonnets have to be read as a narrative of the progress of love."[16] Surely not. Shakespeare has a good claim to being the greatest narrative artist of all time. He has certainly written more narratives than anyone else that have become part of the story store of later times. Had he wished to create a narrative in the sonnets, he could easily have done so. Instead, he conjures up situations that could unleash narrative power, but stalls them, turns them from story to lyric.

Lyrics satisfy without stories partly because of their brevity, because of their intense reflections on focused facets of experience.

But because of their brevity, and their freedom from story, poets often wish to group them together. Lyric collections may or may not have the sort of unity that arranges their facets into something like an insect's compound eye, offering a richer vision than any one part, or like a geodesic dome, offering a far more imposing structure than any one piece. Sonnet sequences, in the wake of Petrarch's *Rime sparse,* could have that sort of unity. But Shakespeare also makes his *Sonnets* kaleidoscopic, trying out small taps or larger jolts from poem to poem, so that themes, moods, or patterns can persist for a time in slight reconfigurations or suddenly drop out of sight behind other themes, moods, or patterns. By the time he had not just the Mistress but also the Fair Youth as the focus of his verse, Shakespeare had a rich array of possible chips, Poet, Youth, Mistress, a wide range of emotions, and a much larger handful of thematic chips, love, friendship, beauty, time, death, art, status. We will turn to several of these in Chapters 6 and 7. But Shakespeare has more to say about love.

Male and Female: A Singular Doubleness

If one of Shakespeare's aims in his sonnets is to make the most of lyric as opposed to dramatic and narrative verse, the sex of the Fair Youth amplifies his opportunities. He can exploit to the hilt the self-sufficiency of a lyric poem and the openness of its resonance with what lies outside it, including the other poems around it. By writing love poems within a set in which, for 126 poems, all those that focus on a specified beloved focus on a young man, Shakespeare can also add a tantalizing doubleness to poem after poem.

Star sonnets like Sonnet 18, "Shall I compare thee to a summer's day?," celebrate love, and the paradox of the intimacy of the lyric voice and the accessibility of that intimacy to any reader: "So long as men can breathe or eyes can see, / So long lives this, and this gives life to thee." Like the majority of poems before the Mistress sonnets, Sonnet 18 does not specify the sex of the beloved. Shakespeare well understood the power of human sexual dimorphism, and that the differences between male and female are key predictors of behavior. He knew that in the absence of other indicators, a poem by a *William* Shakespeare that contains lines like "Shall I compare thee to a summer's day?" would naturally be assumed, in the isolation its memorability repeatedly ensures, to have been written for a woman.

It always *can* be taken that way, and since it is more often read in isolation than in consecutive readings of *Shake-speares Sonnets,* it most often is. But within the volume it also comes immediately after the first seventeen sonnets urging the Fair Youth to breed, and this poem, which notes that "every fair from fair sometime declines," can therefore pick up additional resonances from its context in the sequence. Its closing couplet, affirming the durability of verse and therefore of "thee," echoes the end of the last of the procreation sonnets, "But were some child of yours alive that time, / You should live twice in it, and in my rhyme," but for the first time without any reproach for the addressee's failure to produce children, and with an open expression of admiration of a beauty so intense it is beyond loss ("thy eternal summer shall not fade"). Taken as a poem in the sequence, it extends the poet's admiration and love for the Youth's beauty, and it affirms a timelessness in the intensity of beauty quite at odds with the concern for time in the preceding sonnets.

Yet the sonnet can easily be detached from its context for another, still more open, more universal set of resonances. Just as Shakespeare plays here on the position of the sonnet within its sequence and its detachability from the sequence, he also plays on

LOVE AND TIME: THE YOUTH 103

the specialness of love and yet its specialness *to everyone*. He plays on the fact that a lover, in the full flush of love, feels the beloved is unique, and uniquely important, and deserving of having that uniqueness acknowledged, honored, celebrated; and also on the fact that if this is true for *him* as lover, it will be true for every person in the full flush of love. We can read Sonnet 18 in isolation as a tribute from one lover, an extraordinarily eloquent one, to his sense of the uniqueness of his beloved and as therefore speaking for us all when we are in love. Not for nothing are Shakespeare's sonnets regarded as a *vade mecum* for lovers.[17] And since these are a man's words, without other cues we will take for granted that the beloved is a woman. But if we read the sonnet within the sequence, we must read it as directed to the Fair Youth, to the particular and exceptional individual Shakespeare has addressed or conjured up through all the sonnets so far, and will focus on for over a hundred more—and that means, of course, to a male. And the intensity of feeling remains the same.

A Double Singularity

Other sonnets that follow can also be read either way, like double-faced portrait miniatures swinging about and about in the breeze as they hang from a string.

Let me make it clear that I am not challenging, as Heather Dubrow has, the division into 126 sonnets to or about a Fair Youth, and the next 28 about a Mistress. Dubrow objects to the critical practice of "gendering the addressees even when the texts do not specify whether they are male or female."[18] As Jackson notes, "There are many references to the maleness of the addressee in Sonnets 1–126 and the femaleness of the addressee in Sonnets 127–54, and no contrary indications."[19] That can only be a deliberate decision, and Shakespeare's.

The poet marks the finality of the last of the Youth sonnets, 126, not just by its epilogic tone but also by its peculiar structure: it is not in fact a sonnet, but *twelve* lines rather than fourteen, and in *six* rhymed couplets, rather than alternate-rhymed quatrains, as if to mark its special place as number 126. The Elizabethans regarded the number 63, known as "the grand climacteric," rather than the biblical three-score-and-ten, as the conventional span of years in a human life. Presumably for that reason Henry Constable's *Diana* (1592) and Michael Drayton's *Idea* (1619) each comprised 63 sonnets.[20] Shakespeare, who begins by urging the Youth to make a copy of himself, goes on to write a total of 126 numbered sonnets directed to, or about, the Youth: 63 times 2, as if he himself has provided enough for a full life for the Youth *and* the complete copy the Youth refused to make. Sonnet 126 also anticipates the shift to come by deploying the word "mistress"—for the only time since Sonnet 20 called the Youth "the master mistress of my passion"—in the sonnet immediately before 127 introduces his Mistress in person. And, as we have seen, Sonnet 127 pointedly echoes the opening of Sonnet 1, to honor the opening of a second sub-sequence. *If* we read any sonnet as part of the sequence, then Shakespeare invites us to read each in the first 126 as to or about the Youth, and each of the rest as to or about the Mistress.

I say *the* Youth rather than a youth or youths, although, as recent commentators have noted, the addressee or subject need not necessarily be the same. Paul Edmondson and Stanley Wells question the assumption "that all the poems up to No. 126 are addressed not only to a young man, but to the same young man."[21] More recently Wells repeats that he thinks it a misconception "to believe unnecessarily that all of those with male addressees are addressed to one and the same person."[22] But while these poems *could* focus on a series of youths, Shakespeare never invites that inference. Indeed, he surely knows enough about human nature, and about minds interpreting texts, to know that we will make the opposite inference.

For all we know he may have *written* poems among the first 126 with more than one person in mind, more than one young man, or perhaps, sometimes, with one woman or more in mind. Sonnet 18 could easily have been composed with a woman in view. Sonnet 27,

> Weary with toil, I haste me to my bed,
> The dear repose for limbs with travail tirèd,
> But then begins a journey in my head
> To work my mind, when body's work's expirèd.
> For then my thoughts (from far where I abide)
> Intend a zealous pilgrimage to thee . . . ,

as Wells suggests, "could indeed be the lament of a travelling player who was missing the company of his wife."[23] But for whatever reason he first composed each of his sonnets, Shakespeare then placed 126 in a continuous sub-sequence in which if the beloved's sex is specified it is always male, then followed with another sub-sequence in which if the beloved's sex is specified it is always female. Theoretically, it could be just as possible that different sonnets in the 127–154 range refer to a number of mistresses, some specifically identified as black-haired, some not. But Shakespeare knows what audiences infer from words and texts. Our minds track agents closely, and, unlike computers trying to make sense of natural language, we assume a continuity of personal referents unless the context suggests otherwise.[24] Precisely because Shakespeare avoids names and specifics of place, time, or even sequence, because he focuses on the intensity of the "I-thou" or "I-he"/"I-she" relationships, and because he stresses again and again the constancy of the male beloved—even if there are lapses on both sides—and the inconstancy of the female, he clearly invites and expects us to assume that the Youth and the Mistress remain the same throughout.

When we read the sonnets in sequence, that is. Nevertheless, Shakespeare surely foresaw that some of his sonnets, such as 18 ("Shall I compare thee to a summer's day?"), 29 ("When in disgrace with fortune and men's eyes"), 30 ("When to the sessions of sweet silent thought"), 60 ("Like as the waves make towards the pebbled shore"), 73 ("That time of year thou mayst in me behold"), or 116 ("Let me not to the marriage of true minds"), sing out so splendidly on their own that they would become the anthology pieces they have in fact become, and that many readers would come to know his sonnets precisely by such poems. (In Shakespeare's day highly popular poems circulated in manuscript and were copied and recopied before they found their way into print in collections called "miscellanies" that prefigure modern anthologies.) Like most of the first 126 poems, none of these identifies the sex of the beloved. They can be taken—and repeatedly have been taken—by those who read them apart from the sequence, as written by a male to a female.

In his recent commentary on the sonnets Paterson endorses Dante Gabriel Rossetti's suggestion that "'there should be an essential reform in the printing of Shakespeare's sonnets. After sonnet CXXV should occur the words *End of Part I.* The couplet piece, numbered CXXVI, should be called *Epilogue to Part I.* Then, before CXXVII, should be printed *Part II.* After CLII should be put *End of Part II.*' . . . These divisions are clear enough when you read the Sonnets straight through—but since hardly anyone does, it would certainly improve their navigability."[25] But

Shake-speares Sonnets as the poet had them printed in 1609 offers far more interest, far more shimmer.

To demarcate a separate Part I for Sonnets 1–126 and Part II for 127–152 would be contrary to the surprise each sonnet offers a first-time reader: will it match, contrast, move on, or shift aside from its predecessor? To preannounce the Fair Youth as a constant presence for the first sub-sequence would be to ignore Shakespeare's play with the open situations and open implications possible in lyrics, like the first sonnet we considered, 30, "When to the sessions of sweet silent thought."

We read that deserved anthology piece without reference to the Fair Youth, and indeed to assume him a priori as the constant subject of the first 126 sonnets, as some modern editors and critics tend to do, can rob a poem like this of its power. The Poet's solitary reflections on the sorrows of past losses, on the "precious friends hid in death's dateless night," depends for its impact on the surprise of the introduction, delayed until the last moment, of a "dear friend" unhinted at in the sonnet until now. The poem can work entirely on its own—"friend" could be used to refer to a lover as well as in its modern sense—or it can be read as part of the relationship between Poet and Youth.

The previous sonnet, too, depends for its first impact on *not* being assumed in advance to be addressed to the Youth. In its relationship to Sonnet 30, Sonnet 29 also offers an exemplary instance of the nonnarrative links possible between poem and poem, of the kinds of patterns Shakespeare can compound not only within sonnets but also between them. Adjacent sonnets may stand in pointed opposition (as in the case of Sonnets 24 and 25, discussed in Chapter 6) or, as here, in intricate parallel. Sonnets 29 and 30 treat a similar theme, virtuosically, and in similar but subtly different ways. In both sonnets, the Poet starts in dejection; in both, a transformation in thought and mood occurs when the Poet suddenly thinks of "thee," a "dear friend" in Sonnet 30 but a "sweet love" in Sonnet 29:

When in disgrace with fortune and men's eyes
I all alone beweep my outcast state,
And trouble deaf heaven with my bootless cries,
And look upon myself, and curse my fate,
Wishing me like to one more rich in hope,
Featured like him, like him with friends possessed,
Desiring this man's art, and that man's scope,
With what I most enjoy contented least;
Yet in these thoughts myself almost despising,
Haply I think on thee, and then my state
(Like to the lark at break of day arising)
From sullen earth, sings hymns at heaven's gate.
    For thy sweet love remembered such wealth brings
    That then I scorn to change my state with kings.

Despite their common trajectory, Sonnets 29 and 30 each start in a different kind of darkness: ill fortune, in 29, and melancholy reminiscence, in 30. And each poem experiments in a different way with the delay of the shift in mood, the sudden introduction of and address to the "thee" who allows a new light to flood in: in 29, until the normal sonnet *volta,* at the start of the sestet, but with an abnormally intense and radiant change of mood, and in 30, until the last possible moment, the couplet.

The two poems seem unlinked by narrative: the ill fortune of 29 plays no part in 30, and the aching retrospects of 30 seem related to 29 not by cause and effect but only by contrast with the previous sonnet's mood of apprehensive prospects. But each poem evokes the psychological postulate of the first part of the sonnet with a wonderfully intimate and fresh sense of human truth, even if that initial mood may be, indeed, only a different poetic postulate.

The variation-on-a-theme structure and the lack of narrative links suggest that we should recognize the poems as controlled artistic experiments, rather than direct emotional transcripts, even if in each case the switch in mood comes as a resounding and heartfelt relief, and, once it occurs, seems within the sequence of the whole volume a further tribute to the power of the Youth's image over the Poet's heart and mind. Shakespeare indicates the pointed pairing of these two sonnets by echoing the phrase that introduces the previously unhinted-at addressee: "Haply *I think on thee,*" at the start of 29's sestet, and "if the while *I think on thee,*" at the start of 30's couplet. Narrative makes no sense of this pairing; but as lyric explorations of dark moods and dazzling changes of mood, these two sonnets cast a double spell of poetic magic.

In the same way the next poem in the sequence *after* Sonnet 30 can be read on its own, or seen as an immediate sequel and explanation of the bold claim in Sonnet 30's couplet, "But if the while I think on thee (dear friend) / All losses are restored, and sorrows end":

Thy bosom is endearèd with all hearts,
Which I by lacking have supposèd dead,
And there reigns Love, and all Love's loving parts,
And all those friends which I thought burièd.
How many a holy and obsequious tear
Hath dear religious love stol'n from mine eye,
As interest of the dead, which now appear
But things removed that hidden in there lie?
Thou art the grave where buried love doth live,
Hung with the trophies of my lovers gone,

Who all their parts of me to thee did give,
That due of many, now is thine alone.
    Their images I loved, I view in thee,
    And thou (all they) hast all the all of me.

"All losses are restored" in Sonnet 30, perhaps because in Sonnet 31 all the aspects loved in others are now contained in "thee." The last line of Sonnet 31, striking in its outrageous verbal play on *all* and *thou, they, the, me,* which would make no sense in another context but perfectly clinches the argument here, shows Shakespeare again pushing the patterned play with language and the structure of the single sonnet as far as they will go. At the same time he also probes yet another side of the mystery of love, the curious relationship between the uniqueness of a single love, on the one hand, and on the other this love's capacity to contain elements of the love one has also felt toward others. He can do this as richly as he does by addressing a specific love, or any beloved, or the particular "dear friend" of the previous sonnet and the rest of the sub-sequence.

All through the first 126 sonnets Shakespeare makes the most of the doubleness of sonnets within a sequence: as assigned a fixed place in the sequence or as poems entirely and sometimes triumphantly self-contained. Like many other sonnets, each of the anthology pieces here, addressing only "thee" or "you" or "my love," can seem like an optical illusion, flipping from male to female, as we read it within the sequence or as a lyric standing on its own.

Orientation

Because attitudes to homosexuality have changed so much over the last half-century, much has recently been written about the love that Shakespeare's sonnets express for the Fair Youth. Many have noted that the category "homosexual" was not available in

Shakespeare's time (sodomy, after all, could incur the death penalty), yet the work of his contemporaries Marlowe, Drayton, and Barnfield has strong homoerotic elements. Many have also noted that in Shakespeare's day male-male friendship could be more readily expressed in terms closer to the language of love than most heterosexuals would now feel comfortable with, even in the world of modern "bromance." Shakespeare read Montaigne, whose essay "On Friendship" compares "this brotherly affection with affection for women." Of the latter, Montaigne concedes, "Its ardor, I confess, is more active, more scorching, more intense. But it is a fickle flame, undulating and variable, a fever flame, subject to fits and lulls, that holds us only by one corner. In friendship it is a general and universal warmth, moderate and even." Citing this, Carl Atkins comments that if we see the Poet's relationship to the Youth in the sonnets "as being a recognizable and acceptable one for the time, we may leave concerns about Shakespeare's sexual orientation behind and take from the *Sonnets* what is universal to all loving relationships, heterosexual, homosexual, or passionate friendship."[26] Or, like all the Janus-faced sonnets among the first 126 that we can read as either to a male or to a female, we can see Shakespeare as teasing us with uncertainty: his feelings for the Youth as passionate friendship shading into idealized love, or as something more?

In his edition of the *Sonnets,* Stephen Booth famously wrote that "William Shakespeare was almost certainly homosexual, bisexual, or heterosexual. The sonnets provide no evidence on the matter."[27] I agree. But whether or not Shakespeare was homosexual, he was at least extraordinarily "gay-friendly," as the gay website AfterElton rates heterosexual film directors, like Billy Wilder, who accept rather than mock homosexual love.[28] As Wells reflects: "Shakespeare succeeds in writing verse which, like that of [Marlowe, Drayton, and Barnfield], can certainly appeal to a homoerotic readership but which transcends the boundaries of subdivisions of human experience to encapsulate the very essence of human love. As we might have expected of him."[29] All the more so if we recognize the deliberate and singular doubleness of so many of the most memorable sonnets among the first 126—a doubleness of a kind possible only in lyrics, not in story.

Beyond Love

6

Status

When Shakespeare makes a young man the actual or potential addressee of most of his sonnets, his choice may or may not reflect biographical realities, whether directly or via intermediate mirrors and lenses. But his strategy certainly earns attention by standing out from expectations of sonnet sequences, and it adds a shimmer, a potential doubleness, to sonnet after sonnet. By not specifying a young man as subject or object, many a sonnet seems to invite the heterosexual default reading in isolation but a different response in sequence.

Focusing most of the first 126 sonnets explicitly or implicitly on a male and, often, on a young man of higher rank also allows Shakespeare to complicate the relationship between lover and beloved in standard sonnet sequences. Through the relationship between Poet and Youth he explores other sides than sexual love of our relationships with one another. In Paterson's apt formulation, Shakespeare subverts tradition by focusing, as tradition expects, on love, but then by including everything under that rubric.[1]

Status and Prestige

The poet-lover of most sonnet sequences stands in a relation of subjection to, or even abjection before, the unattainable beloved. As we have seen, sexual difference makes it natural for females to prefer to resist male sexual attention except on their own often highly selective terms, and for males to persist despite, and even because of, resistance—*because of,* since a woman's failure to show her selectivity might call her future fidelity into question. The conventional sonnet sequence captures the logic of the situation: the male demonstrates at once his fitness, his wit, his capacity to outperform rivals, through the ingenuity of the sonnets, but at the same time displays his future commitment as best he can, by expressing in the most extravagant terms his conviction of the unparalleled excellence of the beloved.[2] He will declare her beyond deserving, even as he tries to show by the sheer craft of his verse the depth of *his* desert.

The standard sonneteer emphasizes his abjection, not before other *men,* of course, but only before the woman he loves and serves. Something of this imbalance between Poet and Beloved existed also in the relationship of poet and patron in early modern England, and in shifting from female to male beloved Shakespeare could deploy that similarity to explore equality and inequality in love and beyond.

Some evolutionary analysts distinguish between *status*—the power of compelled dominance, common among animals (think of alpha male chimpanzees and silverback gorillas), the power to assert priority to resources like territory, food, sexual access to females—and *prestige,* freely given recognition, a route to identifying and learning from the most successful in a species like ours, in which social learning matters so much.[3] In early modern England, patrons had high status, both rank and resources, but by bestowing their favors, and their financial support, on those who might earn prestige, they could also earn reflected prestige themselves. Patrons can still do so, of course, but now artists mostly earn their own status—wealth and the power it buys—directly, by means of their capacity to command the attention of others, in a free market of prestige in exchange for payment.

Shakespeare makes the relation of poet and patron a recurrent, though far from a continuous, part of the relationship between Poet and Youth. Status is often not at issue in the sonnets, but wherever it is, the Youth's, the beloved's, tends to be much higher than the Poet's, echoing both conventional sonnet sequences and the relation of poet to patron.

In Sonnet 25 Shakespeare introduces for the first time the idea that his fortunes are low:

Let those who are in favour with their stars
Of public honour and proud titles boast,
Whilst I, whom fortune of such triumph bars
Unlook'd for joy in that I honour most.
Great princes' favourites their fair leaves spread
But as the marigold at the sun's eye,
And in themselves their pride lies burièd,
For at a frown they in their glory die.
The painful warrior famousèd for fight,
After a thousand victories once foiled,
Is from the book of honour razèd quite,

And all the rest forgot for which he toiled:
Then happy I, that love and am beloved,
Where I may not remove, nor be removed.

Saturated though Sonnet 25 is with consciousness of status, the
Poet does not imply here that the one he loves necessarily has a
higher social position. Rather, *unlike* those whose rise in status depends on the fickle favors of rank or fortune, *his,* the Poet's, high
position—in love—is secure: he is exalted in his own way through
the constancy of reciprocated love. He stresses the equality in his
love: though without public honor or proud title, he is loved and
beloved, and may not remove or be removed from that love.

But then in Sonnet 26, Shakespeare considers the converse.
Instead of being never removed from his love, and equal, the Poet
is removed precisely because he is so unequal to the Lord of his
love. He is so low, a vassal before such a lord, that he dare not
even show his face:

Lord of my love, to whom in vassalage
Thy merit hath my duty strongly knit,
To thee I send this written ambassage,
To witness duty, not to show my wit;
Duty so great, which wit so poor as mine
May make seem bare, in wanting words to show it,
But that I hope some good conceit of thine
In thy soul's thought (all naked) will bestow it,
Till whatsoever star that guides my moving
Points on me graciously with fair aspect,
And puts apparel on my tattered loving
To show me worthy of thy sweet respect.
    Then may I dare to boast how I do love thee;
    Till then, not show my head where thou mayst prove me.

Here we hear exactly the note of exaggerated deprecation of self and exaggerated exaltation of the other common in the dedicatory epistles of late Elizabethan poets to their patrons. The language here, as many have noted, echoes Shakespeare's own to the Earl of Southampton, when he sued for the Earl's patronage in the dedication to *Venus and Adonis* in 1593 and when he expressed his fulsome gratitude for Southampton's favor the next year in his dedication to *The Rape of Lucrece.*

But this sonnet seems to have been written some years later,[4] and was certainly published much later, and without any dedication to a patron. Rather than taking the sonnet's subservience to point to some possible biographical narrative, we should note how it embodies actual and immediate lyric artistry. Like Sonnets 29 and 30, Sonnets 25 and 26 have clearly been written to stand as a pair, as well as to work independently. The words "star" (26.9; in 25.1, "stars") and "boast" (25.2, 26.13) occur in both poems, a pairing that occurs nowhere else in the sonnets (and "star" occurs in only four other sonnets, "boast" in only three). The pairing of the two sonnets offers a perfect example of the movement by contraries that Jackson notes as characteristic of the relationship of sonnet to sonnet, as well as of so many individual sonnets, and of Shakespeare's plays.[5] We might note also that the internal contraries that Shakespeare exploits in the multiple plots within his plays also match the external contraries as he alternates from tragedy to comedy over much of his career.

For the first time in the *Sonnets,* the Poet in Sonnet 26 explicitly *writes to* the Youth, as a mere vassal sending nothing less than an "ambassage" to the Lord of his love, a testimony of his fealty that explains his reason for absence. He dare not appear in person, dare not "show [his] head" before his Lord of love because the "wit . . . so poor" in this very note seems "bare," "all naked," "tattered." Instead of being able to write verse capable of immortalizing the Youth, as he could do tentatively in Sonnet 15, confidently in 17, resoundingly and unforgettably in 18, and defiantly in 19, the Poet can only send a humble note expressing his humble obeisance in love ("To witness duty"), while apologizing for a wit so poor that it keeps him from the one he loves.

Nothing in Sonnet 26 explains in narrative terms why the Poet has had a sudden access of incompetence, or at least of a sense of incompetence, or a sense of a need to abase himself before a Youth with whom he has just been on such proudly and securely equal, fully reciprocal, terms in the previous sonnet. Nothing indicates an event, or a series of events, that has led to such emphatic change. The sonnet simply starts from a different position, one of complete abjection, which it takes for granted and states from the first as a given ("Lord of my love, to whom in vassalage . . ."). Again, were Shakespeare trying to tell or imply some narrative, the shift between the positions of Sonnets 25 and 26 would be momentous, and to have failed to account for such a wrench would be a serious failure.

If, on the other hand, we read these two sonnets as lyric explorations of possible relations in love, they make full and satisfying sense. In Sonnet 26 Shakespeare extravagantly expresses a sense of unworthiness before the worthiness of the beloved, a sense of love as complete inequality, in contrast to the equality in love in the previous sonnet. Sonnet 25 says nothing about the status of the beloved: only that the poet is lowly, but that despite that, he is exalted, securely so, because his love is wholly returned. Then Sonnet 26 offers the converse: his beloved is so exalted that the Poet dare not show his face—and even hesitates to write—to the beloved. The intensity of the contrast, the suddenness of Shakespeare's shake-up of the kaleidoscope, should add to our esteem for his lyric imagination, his exploration of the diverse possibilities in love, rather than thwart our thirst for narrative.

As if to confirm the absence of narrative continuity, and the presence of a different kind of imaginative progression, Sonnet 27 ("Weary with toil, I haste me to my bed") follows with none of the sense of inequality between Poet and Beloved in Sonnet 26, but instead picks up on the distance between Poet and Beloved in the earlier sonnet, though now in a purely physical sense. The Poet in bed, "limbs with travail tirèd" (travail: toil *and* travel), finds his thoughts "Intend a zealous pilgrimage to thee": no sense now of reluctance to cross the distance to his beloved. And instead of the emphatic *contrast* connecting 25 and 26, 27 leads into a splendidly close *parallel* in 28, in one of the finest harmonic pairings in the whole sequence. Sonnet 28 cannot stand independently of 27 (it starts by referring directly back to its predecessor, "How can I then return in happy plight"), but it leads in turn into the parallels, and variations on a theme, in 29 and 30, which can and so often do stand on their own.

But so far we have considered Sonnet 26 only in thematic terms: the Poet is physically removed from his Lord of love, and too poor in wit to dare show his face. If we look at the sonnet's poetic texture, however, we can see the poet playing the kind of complex games with status that recur throughout the sonnets, here by toying richly with verbal poverty. Elsewhere, including elsewhere in the sonnets, Shakespeare eloquently and empathically imagines merit nervous before rank, "art made tongue-tied by authority" (Sonnet 66). Here, daunted by his Lord, his very fingers seem to stammer across the page on the far from mellifluous syllable "it," the most commonplace and unprepossessing of English words (merit . . . knit . . . written . . . witness . . . wit . . . wit . . . show it . . . bestow it), a hesitation compounded by other nervous repetitions ("not to show my wit . . . wanting words to show it"), even in the rhyme from the first quatrain weakly carried over into the second ("show my wit . . . show it"). In English verse, repetition of a whole rhyme syllable—extolled in French versification as *rime riche*—is seen as poor rhyming, and the "wit" ending line 4 all but recurs exactly through the slurring of "show it" in line 6, as if in proof of his verbal poverty—but with, all the time, underneath, as Vendler points out, a witty concealment of the word *wit* in the scared witlessness he pretends to ape.[6] Even at a first glance the poet's show of flustered humility takes place within well-formed verse that shapes assuredly its images of fealty and naked poverty; but looked at more closely, the poem displays a dazzling virtuosity that undermines the profession of inadequacy. What does Shakespeare mean by offering in immediate succession two such contrary images, of love as equal, perhaps despite social difference, in Sonnet 25, and love as professedly unequal, but with the inequality covertly undermined, in Sonnet 26?

Lyric "Speech" and Lyric Silence

In the customary "male lover–female beloved" basis of sonnet cycles, there is a natural, easily understood reason for the woman's resistance, and therefore for the man's persistence and his extreme exaltation of the beloved. But the "Friend" he addresses has no reason for resisting, *unless* Shakespeare were proposing a sexual relationship, which as Sonnet 20 playfully makes clear is not the case, despite the depth of feeling. The Poet's persistence in articulating his adulation therefore introduces a frequent instability into the sonnets, an instability that allows him to express the complexities and ambiguities of love and friendship, especially as they relate to status, reciprocity, and fairness.

Here again Shakespeare makes the most of the one-sidedness of the sonnet sequence and of lyric verse in general. He repeatedly addresses a single "thou," from whom we never hear. The absence of dialogue adds to the strangeness of the Poet's persistence when no resistance is voiced or even implied. Shakespeare of course knew well the back and forth of drama, and even his narrative poems offer impassioned argument and counterargument; but here his insistence and the Friend's silence add to the fertile mystery of the sonnets.

Sometimes we can read Shakespeare's obsessive return to his subject as a manifestation of the intensity of his love, whether we read an isolated sonnet, in default mode, as from male to female, or as part of the Poet to Fair Youth sub-sequence. Indeed the male-male relationship can seem even more exalted, since there is no resistance to overcome, no reason other than pure attachment to wish to be near the Friend, nothing like the same reason (potential cuckoldry, the risk of investing resources in a child not one's own) to fear others' interest in a male as opposed to a female friend. Sometimes we can read the poet's deprecation of himself and exaltation of the Friend as poet writing to patron, as middling status deferring to nobility, as advancing age addressing budding or blooming youth, as ordinary looks smitten by the extraordinary, as person extolling paragon.

And often we cannot help reading the instability of the distance between abject Poet and exalted Friend as a way of testing and questioning the mutuality and reciprocal engagement that Shakespeare the dramatist evidently favors in love and friendship: in, for instance, the free give-and-take of young love, expressed in sonnet form, by Romeo and Juliet; in the passionate antagonism-cum-attachment of Beatrice and Benedick; in the luxuriating love-rehearsals of Rosalind and Orlando; in the intimate emotional disclosures of Viola and Orsino; in the mutual commitment of Antonio and Sebastian.

Evolution, Status, and Sociality

Evolutionary biology and psychology have focused intently on the importance of status and prestige, dominance and submission, reciprocity and fairness, in humans, other primates, and elsewhere, with fascinating results that help illuminate the instabilities in Shakespeare's sonnets.

Biologists agree on defining status in terms of priority of access to scarce resources, such as food, territory, and sex. Those terms make clear how closely status can correlate with survival and reproduction (and the survival of offspring to *their* age of reproduction), and therefore how desirable it is, and how likely to be contested, in any species in which status differences exist. In social species with status differences, dominance and submission behaviors evolve to minimize the health and energy costs of constant fighting over resources.[7] The question arises: are humans naturally hierarchical or, like some species, even some primates, egalitarian?

In our case, uniquely, the answer seems to be: both. We have the strong hierarchical streak evident in most primates, and an eagerness for dominance and a readiness for submission manifested even in such contemporary phenomena as democratic politics, celebrity culture, and reality shows. From an early age, even in the nursery and playground, we sense and can squabble over status differences.[8] But we also appear to have passed through a long egalitarian phase, not through our lack of individual desire to dominate others, but through our even stronger *shared* desire not to be dominated. In the hunter-gatherer societies that seem to provide the best approximation of the conditions of human societies in the Paleolithic, egalitarianism rules: the impulse for domination can be kept in check by the concerted effects of all to ensure that no one can dominate others. A moral community, a shared sense of values, allows the weaker collectively to ensure that no strong individuals or coalitions can expect the deference of others.[9]

Such ancestral conditions could change relatively easily once agriculture allowed permanent settlement and concentrations of wealth and therefore power. In these circumstances, hierarchies could reemerge and even become much steeper than in other primate societies. In such cases, especially in early empires, in early modern kingdoms, and even in thoroughly modern instances such as Kim Jong Il and Nursultan Nazarbayev, there can be enormous concentration of power, and exaltation of leaders, and emphatic advantages to being closely associated with those higher in the hierarchy (compare, for the last of these, Sonnet 37: "I am not lame, poor, nor despis'd, / . . . I in thy abundance am suffic'd, / And by a part of all thy glory live"). Nevertheless we retain a strong dislike of being dominated. This has allowed democratic institutions to emerge even in large-scale societies, and values of egalitarianism or counterdominance to inflect even steeply hierarchical relations, as in the professions of egalitarianism of a Kim Jong Il or a Robert Mugabe.

Evolutionary biology has focused on sociality not just in terms of status competition but also in terms of social cooperation. Close cooperation begins with inclusive fitness, or shared genetic interests, first in a mother's concern for her children, or, in the case of species in which the father's presence will improve the offspring's survival rates, in the kind of emotional commitment we know as romantic love, tested, as we have seen, through female selectivity and male persistence. Cooperation expands beyond family relatedness through what biologists call reciprocal altruism, a willingness to repay services, "you scratch my back and I'll scratch yours" (or, for that matter, "you thump mine and I'll thump yours"). This can emerge in relationships in which the overlap of interests is provisional, in creatures that evolve both the cognitive capacity to keep track of debts and favors, and emotions like gratitude, outrage, and a sense of fairness.[10] Friendship on the other hand taps into the same chemical basis (the so-called cuddle chemical, oxytocin) as other forms of attachment, familial and romantic, to create a commitment that does not depend on keeping a tally of services, and that therefore encourages sociality and support even in the least favorable circumstances and therefore when the chances of any repayment of kindness look their worst.[11]

Sonnet 57

How might knowing the deep roots of our social emotions help explain or sharpen our response to a Shakespeare sonnet? Take Sonnet 57:

> Being your slave, what should I do but tend
> Upon the hours and times of your desire?
> I have no precious time at all to spend,
> Nor services to do, till you require.
> Nor dare I chide the world-without-end hour,
> Whilst I (my sovereign) watch the clock for you,
> Nor think the bitterness of absence sour
> When you have bid your servant once adieu.
> Nor dare I question with my jealous thought
> Where you may be, or your affairs suppose,
> But, like a sad slave, stay and think of naught
> Save where you are how happy you make those.
>   So true a fool is love, that in your will,
>   Though you do anything, he thinks no ill.

I have noted that it seems natural for humans both to behave hierarchically, to seek for dominance or act submissively toward the dominant, *and* to resist being dominated if possible. Shakespeare captures the ambivalence here. The speaker can be read as resignedly, devotedly, submissive, or as wishing to resist the inequality

STATUS 127

he is forced into, in a bitterly ironic reproach that nevertheless
dares not speak out directly: the lack of love, as it were, that dares
not speak its name. To my initial surprise, my students almost
invariably take the sonnet at first as a straightforward expression
of the abjectness of devoted love, partly because they can recognize, especially in Shakespeare's work, the figure of the abject lover.
They would not wish to be so abject in love themselves, but they
can readily suppose it would have seemed more acceptable in earlier and more hierarchical times. Such reactions can be seen even
in more sophisticated readers. In response to W. H. Auden's question, "what on earth would you feel if someone handed you [Son-
net 57] and said 'This is about you'?" John Bayley answered, "Rather
gratified, surely?"[12]

Shakespeare allows an abject but accepting reading of the
poem, a reading of the speaker as sufficiently in love to be ac-
quiescent in abuse, but he also surely undermines such a reading.
The lover as slave features sporadically in other sonnet sequences,
even in Shakespeare's own (the Youth in thrall to the Mistress is
a "slave to slavery" in Sonnet 133), but as an image, not a stark
fact, as it is here in the abrupt "Being your slave"—admission,
concession, and declaration, all at once, expanded on and explored
throughout the rest of the sonnet. "What should I do but . . . ?"
seems to accept the condition, but in the spirit of "This is what
you *think* I should be and do, though not what I actually *am* or
do, or what I think I should be or do: merely what I must do, if I
am not to make myself even more unhappy by losing your last
profession of love."

Shakespeare here exploits the gap between ostensible assertion
and the natural inferences, based on shared human feeling, that
count against it. Over the last decade or more, scholars committed to historicism, to ascertaining the unique assumptions of particular periods, have rediscovered the richness of the role of service

in Shakespeare's time, and have shown that service inflected relationships all the way from the lowest servant to nobles serving the monarch, and that it could incorporate affection as well as duty.[13] Shakespeare of course accepts this background of service, rather different from our own greater reliance on often impersonal, and primarily monetary, rewards and our emphatic insistence on autonomy. But I doubt he expects his readers to accept his apparently matter-of-fact "Being your slave." He did not know that anthropologists would discover that hunter-gatherers value autonomy enough to resist anyone in their band trying to assert dominance, but he could intuit human nature by reflecting on himself and others to recognize how much we all value autonomy.

One of the subtlest commentators on the sonnets, John Kerrigan, notes Sonnet 57's "first glint of irony" in line 3, earlier than some other commentators find it.[14] But surely the first irony comes in the first phrase. Shakespeare does not expect us to imagine that he accepts a position as slave, even if the "you" of the poem (itself here a term of deference, rather than the more intimate and equal "thou" the poet uses in most of the sonnets) treats him as one. Shakespeare's own words offer a much closer guide to his thought than the terms others in his time use. If we take only one phrase per play, they include "abhorred slave," "base slave," "damned slave," "devilish slave," "mindless slave," "perfidious slave," "pernicious slave," "rascally slave," "unhallowed slave," "worthless slave," and "wretched slave."

The line Kerrigan singles out as the first glint of irony is "I have no precious time at all to spend"—that is, "till you require." He remarks: "The poet's *time* is not *precious* till spent for the young man . . . yet the adjective is there in any case, suggesting that the poet knows the value of the *time* which he claims he cannot value till his beloved employs it."[15] Indeed. And time is a precious resource for *any* creature, as behavioral ecology shows: time lost to one activity is time we cannot assign to some other activity we may rate as more profitable. That is precisely why attention is at such a premium in consciousness, and why having it usurped in ways we find fruitless or inimical to our own interests so exasperates us. Shakespeare appeals to our common sense of things. Again and again throughout the sonnets he pictures time as an impersonal force affecting us all equally, but here he merely feigns to accept it as something which "you" has at his command, but which does not count for "your servant." A servant, at least, could expect to be rewarded for service, in food, lodging, gratitude, and more. In the world of this painful sonnet, the poet seems to receive nothing in return for devotion but neglect, while nevertheless having to remain perpetually on call.

The sonnet continues with the same ironic force, the same precision of apparent compliance and actual, albeit ostensibly suppressed, anguish. "Nor dare I chide": "I could chide, I want to chide, but I dare not, our relationship is so imbalanced, so unreciprocal." "Nor dare I chide the world-without-end hour / Whilst I (my sovereign) watch the clock for you": throughout the sonnets, the Poet has promised the Youth an enduring, world-without-end immortality, but here he feels his own reward to be no more than having to wait out an eternity alone. "Nor [dare I] think the bitterness of absence sour": "I *feel* the absence bitter, I even use the word, but I *dare* not construe the absence as arising from sourness on your part." "Nor dare I question with my jealous thought": "my thought *is* jealous, but I dare not raise my misgivings even to myself, you have me in such thrall." "But like a sad slave"—as others have noted, the Poet now makes explicit that he knows perfectly well he is *not* a slave, as he professed in the opening phrase, but is merely treated *like* one—I "stay and think of naught / Save, where you are, how happy you make those": "I cannot help thinking of you, wherever you are, choosing not to spend your time with me, but with others, who of course also adore your company, as I do, although I dare not ask to be given the chance to share it." This would be exactly the position of a literal servant, happy to share in the knowledge that his master is entertaining others hierarchically much higher than himself, because the higher the master, the nobler by association the position of his servant, and the more readily the servant should expect to be rewarded (as in Sonnet 37, again: "I in thy abundance am sufficed, / And by a part of all thy glory live"). But *this* servant receives no reflected glory and no reward. (Of course, in other sonnets in the sequence, in other moods, Shakespeare's effects are quite different: the Poet glories in his relation to the loftiness of the Friend.)

As often, the couplet closes and clinches the sonnet with a twist. Love is foolish: love is *so true a fool,* "so loyal to the beloved," *or* "such an utter fool," that "Though you do anything, he thinks no ill." As others have noted, Shakespeare switches from the personal to the impersonal, from himself, loving, to "love," in the third person.[16] He cannot say of *himself,* by now, that he thinks no ill, but he can attribute that folly to "love." Yet as he knows, such a love, such a treatment of one who loves you, without the reason a beloved woman may have for resisting, preserves vanishingly little of love.

In earlier chapters I have referred to the resonance that lyrics can have for receptive readers who respond to the openness of poems unconfined by story. Here in Sonnet 57 we can infer all we need of a situation, and an emotion, an emotion whose very dread of expressing itself overtly to "you" amplifies its impact for *us.* On its own, the sonnet could be directed to either a woman or a man, and the subject could be romantic love or loving friendship. Shakespeare exploits here the full magic of the lyric mode. We overhear a semblance of intimate speech, addressed to one dear other, or perhaps of private thought, the "I" seeming to rehearse what he might dare to say to "you," even as we also recognize a self-conscious poet writing for us, his unseen eavesdropping audience—whom he trusts to be less emotionally deaf, in this instance, than his ostensibly intimate addressee.

The sonnet can resonate for us, for any of us who have ever felt ourselves in a painfully unequal relationship of love or friendship, where we have not been granted the other's time or attention except on the other's whim. And it works, it resonates, through the appeal Shakespeare makes to our sense of autonomy, to our sense of our perfectly natural self-interest in our available time, our thoughts and feelings, to our sense of reciprocity and fairness. Shakespeare trusts enough what we share to assume that we will construe the true feelings he dares not voice to the "you" who still expects he can take the Poet's allegiance for granted.

If we read the sonnet in context, it occurs not as part of a conventional sequence of sonnets to a woman expected to remain conventionally aloof. That convention begins naturally in male-female sexual difference, in the likelihood of male persistence and female resistance. By defying the convention, by confronting us with a unique, individual situation, in which his insistent relationship with the Friend cannot help taking on a new tinge, Shakespeare keeps the feelings fresh, urgent, personal. G. Blakemore Evans in the Cambridge edition of the *Sonnets* warns: "The tone of apparent servility in Sonnets 57 and 58 (a linked pair) is more distressing to a modern reader than it would have been to an Elizabethan, who would have recognised it as part of the conventionally sentimental submissiveness expected of a lover in the sonnet tradition."[17] This unironic reading seems to underestimate Shakespeare's care to question and refresh convention, to probe real feelings, to choose words carefully enough for careful readers of his own or any time to register the sonnet's anguished ambivalence. "Slave" becomes not a conventional sonneteering expression

of abjection, but a word and a situation for him and for us to explore in *this* instance, using all we know of human nature, including the distinction, here pointedly blurred, between the one-sided
relationship of master and slave and the normally or ideally more
reciprocal and affectionate relationship of master and servant.

To read the deep, disturbed ambivalence of this sonnet does
not *require* an evolutionary perspective, but a reading informed
by evolution will be more primed than others today to attend to
the complexities and ambivalences of our readiness for hierarchy
and our resistance to hierarchy,[18] and the interplay of our sense of
autonomy and reciprocity and fairness—although evolutionary
analyses themselves also suggest how finely attuned we all are,
being human, to these things. But an evolutionary reading will
also need of course to be sensitive to the particulars of the text; to
the immediate context (of the paired following sonnet, 58, which
adds "vassal" to "slave" and "servant," and ends "I am to wait,
though waiting so be hell, / Not blame your pleasure, be it ill or
well") and the larger contexts of the sonnets as a sequence and a
tradition; and to the still broader contexts of Shakespeare's own
treatments of slavery, service, and the reciprocity of love and
friendship in his plays (see Richard Levin's cogent arguments
that a writer's own examples, especially in other creative work of
the same genre, provide the surest context);[19] and of what these
suggest Shakespeare thinks about such aspects of human nature
(see Robin Headlam Wells for a refutation of the improbable, but
currently academically widespread, claim that Shakespeare neither had nor valued a sense of human nature).[20] An evolutionary
reading will take note of the assiduous historicist scholarship that
has scoured, for instance, assumptions and conditions about service in Shakespeare's day, but it will tend to see these as local
cultural inflections of a common human nature, not proof of fundamental discontinuities between Shakespeare's time and ours. It

will tend to see the range *within* Shakespeare as the closest guide to his sense of human nature and his sense of what he wishes to appeal to in his audience. It will allow us to let his particulars resonate with our individual experience and both our intuitive and our informed sense of common human nature.

7

Death

We have looked at first things—the kind of Shakespeare sonnet we might first encounter, the sonnet he appears to have written first, the sonnet he placed first in the Mistress poems, the sonnet he finally placed first in the whole cycle. And we have looked at status. Let us now turn to last things. How does status inflect Shakespeare's treatment not just of love but also of death?

In Sonnet 1 we saw Shakespeare opening a cycle of a kind normally focused on love with an emphasis not immediately on love but, surprisingly, on the dangers of death. That emphasis on time and death persists not just in the first 17 sonnets. Throughout the first 126 sonnets, the most significant result of shifting from the expected male-to-female frame to the unexpected male-to-male is that it redirects the options for the Young Man's earning a kind of immortality from producing offspring to inspiring the Poet's art.

From the outset, even before his admiration for the Young Man's looks has been explicitly expressed as love, the Poet has insistently implored him to make copies of himself, to stave off the effects of time and death by what we might now call the genetic route. In conventional sonnet sequences, the sonneteer seems stalled at the stage of the so far unsuccessful but still undaunted wooer of a woman whose beauty has prompted his desire—prompted him, in brazenly biological terms, to try to overcome her resistance to selling her eggs at too low a rate, so that they can together cheat death by producing partial but pleasing copies of themselves. *That* route is blocked for the Poet in his relation to the Young Man, but he *can* help him, in a sense, to produce timeless copies of himself, simply by focusing on him again and again as the in-spiration and model for the ensuing sonnets. If it would be too much to say that this becomes the base theme for the Fair Youth variations, we could identify three linked themes: the power of time and death to destroy beauty, the power of beauty to inspire art, and the power of art to withstand both time and death, that circle around the primary theme of love.[1]

Death was there in the first sonnet we read, in the tears "For precious friends hid in death's dateless night," and in the last we glanced at in Chapter 5, with its insistent "dead . . . buried . . . dead . . . grave . . . buried." It was not there in Sonnets 26 and 57, concerned as they were with the status imbalance between Poet and Friend and, in the later sonnet, the weight it imposes on the great dragging present as he awaits his friend's return: in these poems, the status chip covers the death chip on *these* twists of the kaleidoscope. But in other poems in which status also features, albeit in a different mood, one of happily selfless submission, death can be very much visible, as in the opening of Sonnet 71:

No longer mourn for me when I am dead
Than you shall hear the surly sullen bell
Give warning to the world that I am fled
From this vile world with vilest worms to dwell:
Nay, if you read this line, remember not
The hand that writ it, for I love you so
That I in your sweet thoughts would be forgot,
If thinking on me then should make you woe.

Imagination and Death

In Chapter 1 I stressed the invitation to play and pattern that poets naturally make within the confines of the poetic line. Now I wish to expand on an idea adumbrated there. Play normally takes place only in conditions of security, and pattern provides a means of cognitive channeling for the incessant overflow of potential information. A desire for security and an anxiety at lack of control seem widespread in animals with flexible behavior and complex consciousness. But in humans the capacity for apprehension has swelled to vast proportions.

Imagination appears to have evolved to offer animals an immediate biological advantage: to propose to themselves alternative scenarios for possible action.[2] In most animals with rudiments of imagination, such scenarios presumably involve only imminent possible actions, but the human imagination can stretch much further. The human expansion of imagination—through brain growth, through play, art, language, culture—has made complex long-term strategizing possible, in hunting, harvesting, and even space travel, but it has also had the consequence that our minds can run through a host of possible scenarios, including many swarming with threats, dangers, mishaps. We have more negative than positive emotional systems, because the dangers they alert us to can make a much more rapid and decisive difference to our fitness than positive actions or outcomes. Superstitious and religious attempts to ward off foreglimpsed dangers testify across cultures and for tens of thousands of years to the vivid force of human apprehension.

As our imaginations have expanded, we have also become adept at metarepresentation: at entertaining multiple perspectives and understanding the relationship of one perspective to another, like that of successive moments of our past to each other and to the present or the future, or others' perspective on us or anything else.[3] That wide-ranging imaginative capacity has made it impossible for us *not* to consider the world after our own death. Whatever apprehensions we have about life, we know that we will face a death we probably cannot control and that once dead we will no longer exert *any* control: our bodies will be helplessly subject to whatever forces happen to act upon them. Imagination offers us huge benefits, but at our full human level it also exacts a huge cost. If we can imagine other times and perspectives and possibilities, we can also imagine our own deaths: our absence from the ongoing life we now lead, our physical inertness and decomposition, the possibility of our "spiritual" nonexistence, or a permanent prolongation of the pain and grief associated with dying, or worse.

Archaeological and anthropological evidence suggests humans have been preoccupied for eons with our fate after death. Evidence of grave rituals stretches back tens of thousands of years. Early civilizations show an obsession with the afterlife. The first emperors spent enormous resources trying to ensure their status and comfort after death. Many of the most widespread religions, from Christianity and Islam to Hinduism and Buddhism, place a fundamental stress on the fate of the soul in death or reincarnation: local cultural solutions to the problem of our capacity to imagine death.[4]

In modern secular societies with high longevity, security, and prosperity and specialized medical, palliative, and funerary care, we might think that anxiety about death and about the difference the inevitability of our deaths makes to the sense of our life matters much less. But this is not the case. Research inspired by Terror Management Theory, a kind of empirical existentialist psychology, has shown in surprising detail the substantial effects on our thoughts and actions of our consciousness of death.[5] "Mortality salience," in Terror Management terms, even in unrecognized reminders of death, alters our minds in many specific ways. Even in those who claim to have no lively fear of death, hints of death make them reliably more inclined to seek control, to wish to cling to the values of the community of which they form a part, and to rise in esteem within that community's values. We seem to feel that a commitment to an ongoing collective project and an enduring positive reputation within our society offer us the best stay against the disintegration and oblivion of death. Terror Management Theorists plausibly propose that human existential anxiety is a costly by-product of the advantages of the human imagination and of our capacity to share symbolically with others both our apprehensions in the face of death and the meanings we find in life to resist our lack of dominion over death.

I have suggested that play lies at the origins of art. It allows animals to experiment with degrees of risk in situations of security and control. Art, in its play specifically with pattern, offers us a double measure of control: the activity or the work of art is decoupled or shielded from the ordinary activities of life, as pure play is; and the focus on the pattern helps us learn to navigate through the vast flux of information around us. Most poetry celebrates, at least implicitly, the power poets can exert within the line and often within a larger pattern, like that of the sonnet. The imagination at its freest asserts or at least demonstrates its control, a line at a time, a poem at a time. The line becomes a playpen, a place for the pen of the poet to play with patterns in language and life, a sanctum of control even should the poet choose to address the subject of death and our ultimate loss of control.

Shakespeare's sonnets are a supreme set of exercises in often rather demanding imaginative play, as a consequence of his choice to mine thoroughly literature's lyric rather than its narrative vein. Each sonnet remains a surprise: we can never be sure where it will start, whether very close to the last (as in 27–28 or 135–136) or a vast distance away (as in 25–26 or 145–146), or, after we start it, and even just before it finishes, where its mental leaps will land us. Yet the sonnets to the Young Man not only wind the imagination up tight but also repeatedly foreground what has haunted us since our imaginations became fully human: the ability to foresee the emptiness, the absence, of being dead. They celebrate the imagination, but they also return again and again to the death that darkens it, yet repeatedly in a spirit that celebrates in another way the power of the artistic imagination to outlast death.

Sonnet 81

Sonnet 81 faces death as squarely as any:

Or I shall live your epitaph to make,
Or you survive when I in earth am rotten,
From hence your memory death cannot take,
Although in me each part will be forgotten.
Your name from hence immortal life shall have,
Though I (once gone) to all the world must die.
The earth can yield me but a common grave
When you entombèd in men's eyes shall lie:
Your monument shall be my gentle verse,

Which eyes not yet created shall o'er-read,
And tongues-to-be your being shall rehearse,
When all the breathers of this world are dead.
   You still shall live (such virtue hath my pen)
   Where breath most breathes, even in the mouths of men.[6]

As in Sonnets 57 and 71, we again find the emphatic Petrarchan subjection of the poet and the elevation of the addressee, but with a different mood once more. The poem says little more than "Although I will die and be forgotten, your name will live as long as there are people to read this poem." But it says so again and again in a way that advances the argument toward the triumphant, death-defying affirmation of the final couplet, an affirmation clinched by the high patterning of the final line, "Where breath most breathes, even in the mouths of men": two alliterations on *b* and three on *m,* five words, technically, starting with voiced bilabials, four of them on the metrically stressed syllable; *breath* as noun repeated but pleasingly varied in *breathes* as verb, the two stressed syllables connected by the additional unstressed voiced bilabial of *most;* and the rich consonant cluster ending *breathes* that recurs in *mouths.*

Self-contained pattern like this offers a kind of permanence to outface the disorder of time and death, an order that can resist entropy, as we might say in modern terms. Pattern pervades the poem and structures the sonnet. Not only does each line serve as a unit of thought, but so does each pair of lines, and so does each of the first three quatrains. Indeed, each pair of the first eight lines alternates between the survival of "you" (in life or memory) in one line and the oblivion awaiting "me" in the other, starting with the stark *Or* [= *Either*]/*Or* opening of the first couplet. Verbal patterns compound the structural patterns: *I-me-my/you-your* contrasts fill the poem, as do *live* and equivalents *(life, survive, breathe)* and *die* and equivalents *(in earth, rotten, death, grave, entombed).* Other patterns of verbal and phrasal repetition also abound: *shall live* (1, 13); *earth* (2, 7); *from hence* (3, 5); *all the world* (6), and *all the breathers of this world* (12); *men* (8, 14); *eyes* (8, 10); *breathers, breath, breathe* (12, 14).

In order to maximize pattern, Shakespeare does not hesitate to flout normal expectations of English, as in line 11, "And tongues-to-be your being shall rehearse." Until the twentieth century, poets writing in English have rarely thought twice about disturbing the language's increasingly less flexible word order for the sake of the most prominent pattern in English verse, rhyme: here, the inversion in "your being shall rehearse" to obtain a rhyme with "verse." So far, so normal. But Shakespeare also violates idiom here, "rehearse your being" having to mean, in context, something like "repeat aloud the account of your life in this verse monument to your having existed" (isn't it a miracle that readers can construe so much from so little, and that Shakespeare knows we can?),[7] with *rehearse* being chosen not only for the rhyme but also for the additional pun on *hearse,* to join the pattern of other spaces linked with death: *in earth, grave, entombed, monument. Your being* itself ignores usual idiomatic constraints—it does not usually mean "your having been," let alone "this account of your having been"— partly for the sake of the pronounced patterns of alliteration and assonance in *to*NGu*es-to-*BE *your* BE*i*NG. *Tongues-to-be* itself stretches idiom far beyond expressions like "bride to be," partly by way of a bold synecdoche (part for whole), the highly concrete *tongue* for "person" (although the *tongues* will themselves also literally *rehearse* this verse monument to "your" existence). "Tongues-to-be" offers a particularly striking, vividly visceral prophecy of those to come who will read of "you" even "When all the *breathers* of this world are dead"—another Shakespearean transgression of verbal norms, another coinage, not only emphasizing how this verse will outlive everyone now alive, but also stressing the pattern of *mouths* that leads from "tongues-to-be" through "Where *breath* most *breathes*" to the final resonant "in the *mouths* of men."

Shakespeare's insistent play with pattern invites us to play along, within the line, between line and line, within the poem as a whole. His artistry, his boldness, and his assertion of the power of art to outface and outlive the disintegrations of death, depend on his mastery of pattern, on the sense that, here at least, he, and we, can make and multiply sense.

Love, Death, Art

In general when lyrics do not focus on love, and sometimes even when they do, they often focus on death. In the absence of stories, lyrics often make the most of human feeling by the poet's or an imagined speaker's direct appeal to an absent beloved. Even that absence of a beloved can stress the fundamental solitude of the poet's self, or any self, in the face of death. Or poets may use the absence of stories in lyrics to explore the private space left for reflection, and perhaps to muse on their own isolation at its most emphatic, in death—as so frequently and so memorably in Dickinson.

Lyrics so often address death not only because of the solitariness of the poet in composing the poem—not evident in narrative, where writers tend to efface themselves into virtual witnesses to or windows onto others' stories—but also because of the solitariness of the reader. Without stories, lyrics tend to be brief and to compensate for the absence of plot interest by the emphatic presence of verbal novelty and design. Such brief and intensely patterned poems invite readers to become rereaders, to turn back and back again, so that, in a sense, time stands still. The poems that keep readers returning offer a perfection of design, an assurance of control, a guarantee of endurance that seem the converse of the disintegration and the oblivion of death.

On only one occasion in his sonnets (Sonnet 146) does Shakespeare focus on the consolation religion can provide us in our apprehensions about death. Everywhere else love or art, the art of these poems, offers the consolation.

Immortality and Status

In Sonnet 81 and elsewhere we can see not only the play with pattern in Shakespeare's art, and our human desire to cope with our ineluctable awareness of death, but also, once again, his toying with our intense consciousness of status, and our deep-rooted desire to resist the dominance of others. The universal human pattern of counterdominance, of our wishing to assert our rights, where we can, in the face of the dominance of others, wryly inflects this poem as it does so many of the sonnets. Shakespeare may profess his nothingness beside the Fair Youth, but although he writes "Your name from hence immortal life shall have," he never names the young nobleman, while *"Shake-speares Sonnets"* on the title page and every opening of the first edition proclaims the name of the author of this "gentle verse."[8] He knew that this poem would mean his name "still" should live "Where breath most breathes, even in the mouths of men."

This leads us to wider topics. As we saw in the previous chapter, our forebears seem to have passed through a stage when, although we had earlier been accustomed to the primate norm of accepting dominance hierarchies, we began to avoid *being* dominated by acting together to resist the attempts of others to dominate us. This resistance to domination remains part of our psyche, albeit inflected enormously differently from culture to culture. We may wish to impress others, but we also resist our peers' obvious

attempts to impress us, and therefore, although we may strive for
status, we will also be inclined not to flaunt it, or demand its recognition, in front of others. Boastful hunters in hunter-gatherer societies are swiftly mocked; boasters in our own societies may not
always be mocked to their faces—we accept hierarchy more than
hunter-gatherers do—but we may mock them behind their backs
or in the safely sealed court sessions of private thought.

Again and again throughout the sonnets Shakespeare affirms
their power to outlast time and death. But he does so less in explicit
advertisement of his own power, even in the most magnificently
proud of these sonnets, than by affirming the enduring memory of
the one he chooses to immortalize:

> Not marble, nor the gilded monuments
> Of princes, shall outlive this powerful rhyme;
> But *you* shall shine more bright in these contents . . .
>   (Sonnet 55: emphasis added)

Here in Sonnet 81, he affirms "such virtue hath my pen," not as a
direct boast of the immortality awaiting *him* as poet, but in affirming "You shall live . . . even in the mouths of men." About
his own fate he could hardly be more emphatic: "in me each part
will be forgotten"; "I (once gone) to all the world must die," "The
earth can yield me but a common grave."

The stance of self-deprecation before the beloved makes one
kind of sense when a poet persists, sonnet after sonnet, in addressing a steadfastly resistant woman: he hopes to convince her that
his unwavering admiration for a creature so far above him vouches
for his eternal commitment. Shakespeare adopts the same stance
of self-deprecation, not unaware, presumably, that it makes a very
different kind of sense when addressed to a man whose friendship
or love he needs no persistence to win. He professes that the

beauty and the immortality of his sonnets owe everything to the young man's merits, not his own. Yet we see for ourselves the beauty of the sonnets, and can linger over their charms, while we know nothing of the beauty of the young man—fair hair aside— except as it is reflected, very obliquely, in the Poet's enthusiasm.

We read the Poet's "in me each part will be forgotten" knowing that the "you" of the poem has been forgotten, if he ever existed, except in these sonnets, but that Shakespeare's name remains very much alive, and that he could foresee exactly this, even if he professes the contrary. We read his affirming the *Youth's* immortality and *his own* oblivion not as hypocrisy but as pride— perfectly justified—concealing itself in modesty, veiling itself out of deference not only to the Young Man, real or not, but rather more toward us as readers.

Shakespeare knows that we can feel deeply moved, we can feel awe and uplift, before human greatness, even before mere fame or power, but can resent those who strive too single-mindedly for status at the expense of others or try to exact recognition of it from others.[9] Yet if he does not *solicit* our acclaim we will happily *bestow* our admiration freely.

In asserting the immortality that his art can bestow on the young man, Shakespeare resoundingly affirms the power of art at its best. And at its best *his* art invites us to return again and again to his sonnets. We can feel the thrill of participating individually *and,* whether actually or imaginatively, sharing our reactions with others, in the activity of an art that really does allow human works and the responses they evoke to last long beyond our individual deaths. As we noted earlier, in the first sonnet we read, an essential part of the slow spell of a great lyric is its capacity to activate our metarepresentational mind, our ability to hold in mind our own reactions now, and our previous reactions, and the imagined reactions of others, and the poet's inferred anticipation of these reactions. As we savor the sonnets' intricacies of form and complexities of experience, we can have a sense of sharing not only in a physical here and now but in a world of human thought and feeling that extends back into the past and on into the future and to some degree defies time.

That sense will not keep us literally alive, any more than passing on our genes, "mak[ing] thee another self" (10.13), can do, but it makes the most of the imagination that awakens us to the inevitability of our individual deaths. It makes us feel that we belong to something human much larger than ourselves, that art can connect us with one another across time, and can therefore offer consolation and an incentive to future human achievement.

"Increased mortality salience," in Terror Management Theory terms, tends to make us cling more tenaciously to the values of our group and to think more anxiously about our status within what our group values.[10] That can lead to our clinging to parochial values, or to our desire to leave behind marble or gilded monuments or insipid funerary verse, but at its best our awareness of death can have an enhancing effect: a readiness to value and see our own part in what all humans at their best can achieve, a sense that we belong to something much larger than ourselves, a sense of the scope of human powers at their best, in a Sappho, a Rumi, a Shakespeare, or an anonymous Tamil poet, a sense of the connectedness we can have in attuning ourselves to the exact surprises of feeling and form that writers prepare for readers in their time and place and beyond.

We feel proud to be part of a species that can produce a Shakespeare, yet we also have an ingrained resistance to those who assert their own merits and, implicitly, their right to high status, to our deference, our awe, our submission before their genius. Genius stretches human possibility, and puts us in touch both with extraordinary minds and with the ordinary minds of other audiences across time, but it also builds on accumulated human tastes and traditions, and depends for its impact and importance on minds like ours. In his self-abasement before the Fair Youth, Shakespeare seems to recognize the strange democracy and the strange aristocracy of art: he repeatedly wields his verbal might, but removes any sense of arrogating it to himself.

Shake-speares Sonnets, 1609

8

Lyric and Narrative

Eliminating Story

Most lyric poems incorporate—how could they not?—elements of human experience also found in narrative: situations, attitudes, emotions, memories, propositions, settings, characters. Some lyrics may also include simple events—like Wordsworth's sighting "a host of golden daffodils" in "I wandered lonely as a cloud"—usually as subjects for reflection rather than as part of a sequence of events. To the degree that poems incorporate the singular sequences of events characteristic of story, and depend for their impact on these sequences, we regard them as verse narratives rather than lyrics.

In his sonnets Shakespeare avoids narrative and drama, even as he exploits to the utmost the resources of lyrics, individually and in sequence, including the resources that tap, in especially charged ways, into the emotional power that both narrative and drama draw on. While he keeps his lyrics free of narrative he takes full advantage of the intensity of emotional engagement allowed by two love relationships—one more, indeed, than in other Elizabethan sonnet sequences. His focus on love, standard in sonnet sequences, and his cast of defined characters, loving Poet, beloved and idealized Fair Youth, and desired but demonized Mistress, lay the basis for the passionate feeling and thought that he maximizes throughout the sequence. The sustained focus on first the Youth then the Mistress also reduces the costs for us as readers: although Shakespeare may surprise us with shifts in emotion, ideas, and strategies from sonnet to sonnet, we do not have to grope anew for the subject as we do in a collection of a poet's unrelated lyrics. Wordsworth describes this effect well, in introducing his own *Ecclesiastical Sonnets* (1822): "For the convenience of passing from one point of the subject to another without shocks of abruptness, this work has taken the shape of a series of Sonnets."[1]

But the continuity of focus does not mean narrative continuity. Shakespeare does not tell a story, or stories, in his sonnets. He eschews specific narrative details like settings and actions, and not only does he not spell out sequences but he thwarts attempts to infer them. Neither at the beginning of each sub-sequence, nor in later retrospection, does he recount the origin or development of his love for Youth or Mistress. Not until Sonnet 10 does the Poet first say explicitly "for love of me," but intensity of feeling for and intimacy of association with the Youth have run through the preceding sonnets right from the address to the "tender churl" in Sonnet 1. Sonnet 127 introduces "my mistress" with no sense that the relationship is new. And at the end of each sub-sequence the Poet's love continues, whether or not in accord with his better judgment.

Disenchantments occur in both relationships. They persist in the sonnets to the Mistress, although a bitter love or a rank desire remains; but in the Fair Youth sonnets disenchantments—at the Youth's "sensual fault," his relationship with the Mistress, his neglecting the Poet while enjoying others, his relationship with the Rival Poet(s), an apparently final farewell, or disloyalties or infidelities on both sides—seem repeatedly erased from the record and from memory, with unblemished love restored, only to return in another form and then to be erased again, with no sense of continuous cause and effect or cumulative impact.

After the intimation of a cooler mood in the Fair Youth in Sonnets 33 and 34, and of some kind of betrayal by him in 35, and the recognition in the sonnets from 40 through 42 that the Youth has "taken" a woman whom the Poet loves, for instance, the Poet can still write lines like "But you like none, none you for constant heart" (53), as if nothing has happened. Indeed in such later sonnets, those earlier (or at least previously mentioned) circumstances simply play no part, in *these* shakes of the kaleidoscope. Sonnet 87 may seem to mark the end of the relationship, or at least the Poet's rueful recognition that he has reached the end—"Farewell, thou art too dear for my possessing"—but a few sonnets later he can write, as if this has always been the case:

> . . . having thee, of all men's pride I boast,
> Wretched in this alone: that thou mayst take
> All this away, and me most wretched make. (91)

Three sonnets in succession, 94 through 96, reproach the Youth for festering sins or faults, but Sonnet 105 declares, with no shadow of such qualms:

> Kind is my love today, tomorrow kind,
> Still constant in a wondrous excellence
>
> . . . .
>
> "Fair, kind and true" is all my argument.

In view of the evidence that Shakespeare himself arranged the sequence we find in *Shake-speares Sonnets,* the absence of narrative within every sonnet up to the final two (for which, see below), and his demonstrated flair for narrative throughout his plays and narrative poems, we can only conclude that here he sought to frustrate narrative in order to demonstrate the power that his verse could have when free of story.

Triangles

Even the details of the most specific developments, the possible infidelity of Youth and Mistress, and the parallel "infidelity" of Youth and Rival Poet(s), remain unclear. The affair, if it is that, between Fair Youth and Un-Fair Mistress may seem especially at odds with the claim that Shakespeare eschews narrative in the sonnets. But the evidence of the sonnets that focus on this triangular relationship suggests that Shakespeare's interest is not in narrative but in other kinds of pattern, emotional, verbal, and structural.

The first sonnet that refers to what may be the relationship between Fair Youth and Mistress seems uninterested in sequence, but urgent with dramatic immediacy and obsessed with other forms of pattern, verbal as well as emotional:

Take all my loves, my love, yea, take them all:
What hast thou then more than thou hadst before?
No love, my love, that thou mayst true love call:
All mine was thine before thou hadst this more. (40)

After three sonnets on this theme, 40–42, the subject disappears, not influencing the Poet's subsequent relations with the Young Man. It reemerges in the Mistress sequence, in another three sonnets, 133–134 and 144, which treat the theme, once again, without an interest in sequence and produce no narrative consequences in the other Mistress sonnets. I wonder indeed whether the three-way love relationship determines that in each subsequence, to the Youth and to the Mistress, there are exactly three sonnets on the theme.

Shakespeare chooses not to decide what has happened. After sonnets that seem to imply a full sexual relationship, the last apparently referring to the love triangle ends with the Poet acknowledging that he knows nothing definite of what has happened between Youth and Mistress, for all his vivid imaginings:

> But being both from me, both to each friend,
> I *guess* one angel in another's hell:
>   *Yet this shall I ne'er know, but live in doubt,*
>   Till my bad angel fire my good one out.
>   (144.11–14, emphasis added)

As James Schiffer observes, "critics are not unanimous about whether the young friend has a sexual relationship with [the Mistress] as well."[2] All six "love-triangle" sonnets passionately engage the poet in the moment, but defy any attempt to define actions or sequences, and have no consequences in subsequent sonnets.

On a larger scale, nothing in the Youth and Mistress subsequences allows us to say whether the Poet's love for Youth or Mistress began first. Such lack of concern for sequence in the work of a great storyteller can only indicate his *wanting* not to tell a story, even while as a poet he seeks to animate the emotions of love and jealousy with maximum immediacy and resonance. Shakespeare handles Fair Youth and Un-Fair Mistress in ways that reflect his fascination here, as lyric poet, with *non*causal pattern. The Poet's two "loves" are *parallel,* as loves, and as "fair" at least in the sense of their physical beauty. They are also *contrasts*, man versus woman, fair versus dark, idealized versus demonized. And they also *intersect* when they become lovers, if that indeed is what happens.

Their affair, or whatever it is, introduces a theme of rivalry into the Poet's emotional life: the Youth is a rival with him for the Mistress, not that he cares greatly about that; and the Mistress is a rival with him for the Youth, about which he cares a great deal—another pointed parallel and contrast. That jealousy toward a rival in turn generates another structural opportunity, in the Rival Poet(s) sequence, as Jackson notes: "It is thoroughly characteristic of Shakespeare, with his sense of contrast and structural opportunity, to dichotomize the conventional love object into Fair Youth and Dark Woman, create a love triangle in which each becomes the Poet's rival for the other's favour, and then augment rivalry in love with rivalry in poetry."[3]

The Youth's excellence arouses the Poet's love, and his desire to extol him in verse. That very quality—including the Youth's high social position—also inspires other poets (or perhaps just one other) to extol the Youth in their (or his) verse, to seek his patronage, by unseemly flattery if need be, thereby generating in the Poet feelings of jealousy, betrayal, contempt, and inadequacy, as well as confidence in his own plain, unfeigned, and unforced devotion.

The Poet's very concession, "I grant thou were not married to my Muse" (82.1), highlights how the Poet-Youth-Rival(s) sub-sub-sequence, 78–87, matches the jealousy in the Poet-Youth-Mistress sub-sub-sequence: the Poet feels it as "as a kind of infidelity or promiscuity."[4] But the Rival Poet(s) sub-sub-sequence does not decide what prompts the Poet's sense of betrayal: *many* poets writing in praise of the Youth ("every alien pen," 78.3; "they," 82.9; "others," 83.12, 85.13) or a single daunting talent ("a worthier pen," 79.6; "a better spirit," 80.2; "his great verse," 86.1)?[5] Again, the emotion matters, and its immediacy in its moment, rather than some concrete narrative situation that has triggered it, and again, the emotion, however engendered, has no further consequences beyond this sub-sub-sequence.

Intensities and Intimacies

Unlike Petrarch or his own contemporaries, Shakespeare avoids narrative not only from sonnet to sonnet but also within individual sonnets, with the marked and pointed exception of the last two, Sonnets 153 and 154, which form a segue into the narrative and dramatic form of "A Lover's Complaint." Except for these tailpieces, his sonnets eschew specific situations and defined events. And even in these tailpieces, by telling the same miniature myth twice over, in two consecutive sonnets linked by the same first rhyme-word, Shakespeare suggests he has less interest here in narrative progression than in other kinds of pattern, a different slight tap of the kaleidoscope, like the theme and variation in the first seventeen sonnets.

Unlike other sonneteers, Shakespeare also avoids dramatic form, the direct presence and speech of the beloved in specific scenes. The closest he comes is the *recurrent* scene of his Mistress playing the virginal: "How oft, when thou, my music, music play'st / Upon that blessèd wood" (128.1–2). He never cites the beloved's words, although he may refer to what the beloved says in typical and unparticularized terms: "When my love swears that she is made of truth, / I do believe her though I know she lies" (138.1–2).

But while forfeiting narrative and drama in order to explore and exploit what lyric can do, Shakespeare does not forfeit the force of human emotion that both build on. Narrative and drama reach their peak in the intense engagement of person with person, especially in moments of maximum emotional closeness or distance, of amity or enmity. In Shakespeare's sonnets, love supplies the closeness, complicated and often intensified by literal distance. Sometimes physical distance only augments the love, but sometimes love can be racked and riven by emotional distance too, as in Sonnets 57, "Being your slave, what should I do but tend / Upon the hours and times of your desire?"; or 87, "Farewell, thou art too dear for my possessing." For Shakespeare, the beloved always remain physically absent when he writes—in keeping with the sonnets' intense verisimilitude, for if Youth or Mistress were there, he would have other ways to relate to them[6]—yet so emotionally present that he cannot help directing his thoughts and words to them, and not in spontaneous speech but with the brooding effort and passionate care of a poet's craft.

One of the strengths of lyrics can be their intimacy, their sense of immediate engagement with a poet's mind: in Shakespeare's case, the mind of the poet at its most engrossed precisely because focused on, and often addressing, a beloved but absent other, rather than feigning a live exchange. With the other absent as he writes, he has time to bring thought and feeling to white heat in the crucible of his art. Absent in space, but present in thought and time: Shakespeare thrusts us into his immediate present, an extended present of passionate poetic expression, not the relentless moment-by-moment advance of drama's actions and immediate reactions or the compressed former presents of narrative retrospection.

For us to have the sense of privileged access to the poet's mind, to have the impression, in Wordsworth's terms, that we witness Shakespeare unpacking his heart,[7] we need to sense that we encounter no stylized Poet, no parrot of poetic convention, but Shakespeare himself feeling real emotions toward two real people

he loves. He does all he can to generate that sense, and he succeeds. Frederick Furnivall, writing in 1877, speaks for many: "I
could not have conceived that poems so intensely and evidently
autobiographic and self-revealing . . . could ever have been conceived to be other than what they are, the records of his own
loves and fears."[8]

Robert Crosman helps explain this effect: "Too elusive to count
as reliable history, the sonnets also do not give the kinds of signals
that would proclaim them as fiction."[9] Shakespeare names neither
Youth nor Mistress, as if to protect actual individuals, and "as if
to launder them of allegorical fictiveness."[10] He could not be further from the sonneteers of his time, who evoke and address idealized Coelias or Fidessas.

Nothing detracts from the sense that he writes in his here and
now, even if he withholds any details of the here and now—
except for introducing his own name, Will, and referring to his
own life as poet and player.[11] Crosman comments that this

> is a giant step closer to autobiographical intention than is Sid-
> ney's persona. . . . If the poet in Shakespeare's sonnets may not
> be taken as a self-portrait, then it is hard to know who he *can* be.
> It would be a kind of blindness or ideological rigidity on our part
> to deny him that identity, even as it would be naive to insist that
> the insight the sonnets give us into its speaker is a complete and
> accurate historical record. The sonnets are too rich and ambigu-
> ous to count as history, but they are something as good or better—a
> portrait of the artist as lover, painted by his own hand.[12]

Crosman also observes:

> If the framework is not autobiographical, then it mimics auto-
> biography uncannily—or mimics the materials out of which
> autobiography is made: letters and journal entries. The sonnets
> record constant revisions of attitude, as if in response to day-to-
> day events. They predict their own future course poorly, return to

topics already covered as though they were new, shift directions suddenly, and leave gaps unexplained. Most of them, like private letters, neglect to state background information that any reader other than the young man needs to know.[13]

Like other sonneteers, Shakespeare presents himself as unable to help loving, but unlike them he does not love idealized icons, plaster saints, conventional paragons of aloof chastity. The very uncomfortableness and atypicality of the relationships,[14] the sense that the poems are almost torn out of him by his feelings,[15] his apparently being deceived in some poems and deceiving himself there or in others, all seem to vouch for their authenticity.[16] Smitten by lust for the Mistress and by love for the Youth, he cannot withstand the attraction in either case, yet cannot maintain the conviction that the other is perfect or the pretense that he himself has never strayed. He knows his Mistress from almost the first to be untrue, yet he cannot switch off his desire. He knows his love for the Youth remains sexually out of bounds, but he cannot help feeling full-blown love, even when this model of the "Fair, kind, and true" (105.9) proves unkind and untrue or when he himself somehow betrays the Youth emotionally. He does not spell out the offense each may have caused the other, because, implicitly, each already knows precisely the grounds for grief.

Shakespeare's stratagems seem simultaneously to authenticate the relationships and to imply a personal narrative, "so that an overwhelmingly biographical reaction is set up in the reader,"[17] while thwarting narrative so as to amplify the resonance lyric invites. Again and again a sonnet can make us feel that something emotionally momentous has happened, whose hue and valence we can also feel, even if the details remain privy to Poet-Lover and Beloved; as a result, the emotions and their eloquent expression can reverberate all the more in the echo chamber of our own experience. G. K. Hunter suggests that "the reader naturally supplies from his imagination a complete dramatic situation."[18] In fact we never have enough information to infer an imagined scenario, but what we *can* do is feel the poem's emotional force-field even without situating it in specific circumstance.

Although and because his sonnets do not spin stories or stage dramas, Shakespeare awakens in us a sense of access to his private self in the very throes of loving thought. No wonder that readers have craved to know the identities of Youth and Mistress, scholars have scoured so assiduously for biographical evidence, and editors have endlessly sought, equally in vain, to rearrange the sonnets into a single narrative sequence.

Shakespeare draws on the strengths of fiction, engaging elemental emotions from unexpected angles, but adds the apparent charge of the real, the personal and the present, to create also something of the live presence of drama and the privileged intimacy of confession. As Hunter writes, the effect "is that of immediate contact with the suffering mind."[19] And if, as I suspect, the sonnets do not arise directly out of experience with a single fair youth and a single un-fair mistress, that does not make them "literary exercises," let alone "mere exercises."[20] There is nothing *mere* about Shakespeare's being able to conjure up the charge of intense, real, personal experience *and* simultaneously to raise the artistic magic of formal lyric to the highest level.

Pattern outside Narrative

Shakespeare evokes in us a sense of our "immediate contact" with his "suffering mind" but does so without offering a defined sequence of events. By avoiding the linearity of narrative, he can give voice to the fluctuations and repetitions that we recognize in our own emotions and ruminations—in the Fair Youth sequence, for instance, the intermittent oscillation between serenity and alarm or between pride and abjection—rather than being confined by the sustained trajectory of emotions a plot tends to require. He can explore the emotional patterns of love, in its constancy and change, but also leave space for all kinds of other lyric patterns, both within individual poems and within the sequence. Narrative offers us a robust and fertile mode of thought, but causality nevertheless constrains. In the sonnets Shakespeare seems to examine the freedom and openness of thought by eschewing narrative and by allowing full scope to other modes of thought like comparison, analogy, abstraction, and argument. Both through the intricate texture of the sonnets and through explicit claims for the immortality of his verse, he also accentuates the power of craftsmanship and its capacity to step outside, to some extent, the pressures of ongoing time.

I have proposed that we understand art as cognitive play with pattern. Shakespeare in the sonnets avoids the patterns of narrative in order to play most freely with patterns of other kinds, both within and between sonnets: words, images, sounds, structures; emotions and moods, of course; comparison, analogy, abstraction, argument; natural rhythms, in daily, seasonal, and life cycles; repetition, variation, continuity, discontinuity, comparison, contrast, reversal, contradiction, negation, reaffirmation, reconciliation, conjunction, incorporation, exclusion, complication, simplification, intensification, relaxation—all singly or in combination.[21]

In narrative, patterns tend to converge, as succession and causality dominate and direct other patterns of events, characters, and emotions. In the absence of narrative, the proliferation of patterns upon patterns that Shakespeare incorporates into the sonnets—some local, some long-distant, some temporarily dominant, others recessive, or counterpointed—makes the detection of pattern an ongoing pleasure, a hide-and-seek game. In Jackson's terms:

"the sequence is ordered so as to provoke our cooperation in the business of discovering pattern."[22] The proliferating patterns can entice us to reread the sonnets both for the renewed appreciation of patterns already noticed and for the detection of patterns not yet consciously recognized. In that sense the poems keep themselves alive, as they promise they will, challenging the master-narrative of time as death and decay by asserting their own immortality.

Sonnet 18: Connection and Isolation

Sonnet 18 can stand as an example of the kinds of patterns Shake-speare incorporates within and between sonnets:

> Shall I compare thee to a summer's day?
> Thou art more lovely and more temperate:
> Rough winds do shake the darling buds of May,
> And summer's lease hath all too short a date;
> Sometime too hot the eye of heaven shines,
> And often is his gold complexion dimmed,
> And every fair from fair sometime declines,
> By chance or nature's changing course untrimmed:
> But thy eternal summer shall not fade,
> Nor lose possession of that fair thou ow'st;
> Nor shall Death brag thou wander'st in his shade,
> When in eternal lines to time thou grow'st.
> So long as men can breathe or eyes can see,
> So long lives this, and this gives life to thee.

Like so many of the sonnets, Sonnet 18 refers to some of the key patterns in time that we use, both practically and poetically, to understand our life: day and night, the seasons of the year, life and death. Here, Shakespeare compares "thou" both to a summer's day and to summer as a season. Or rather, he *contrasts* a natural summer's day or season, or even the cycle of life and death, in lines 11–12, with the "eternal summer" awaiting "thee" as the subject of this poem. That assertion of the eternal ties this poem tightly to the preceding poems, 15–17, with their introduction of the subject of immortality through verse. Sonnet 18 splendidly fulfills the promise of immortality: Shakespeare surely knew that the radiance of this straightforward and sunny sonnet would make it live.

Its very radiance also connects it by contrast to the sonnet that follows, 19, "Devouring Time, blunt thou the lion's paws." Where Sonnet 18 is supremely gentle and tender, as if spoken to "thee," Sonnet 19 is dark and dangerous, a challenge directed at Time itself. Yet despite that contrast of mood and tone it ends with a couplet that offers another affirmation of the sentiments expressed in the couplet of Sonnet 18: "Yet do thy worst, old Time: despite thy wrong, / My love shall in my verse ever live young." These kinds of contrasts and echoes *between* sonnets (note that these two sonnets also have "lives . . . life" and "live" in their resounding last lines) amplify the patterns *within* the sonnets.

The question Sonnet 18 opens with, "Shall I compare," and the implicit answer, "No, I will contrast," also link with other patterns. Analogy itself is a kind of pattern, matching certain features of the source (in this case, "thou") in one domain to the target (here a summer's day, a summer season) in another. Other sonnets can turn analogical comparison itself into a subject of scrutiny, as in Sonnet 21:

> So is it not with me as with that Muse,
> Stirred by a painted beauty to his verse,
> Who heaven itself for ornament doth use
> And every fair with his fair doth rehearse,

Making a couplement of proud compare
With sun and moon, with earth and sea's rich gems. . . .

Notice here in "every fair with his fair," an echo of Sonnet 18's
"And every fair from fair," as well as the *compare* in both sonnets
(18.1, 21.5). Shakespeare surely intended the wry wit of, or the proto-
Whitmanesque embrace of contradictions in, his offering a brilliant comparison in Sonnet 18—or rather a contrast, since summer
or a summer's day, though proverbially perfect,[23] has nothing like
the perfection of "thee"—and then rejecting the falsity of poetic
comparisons in Sonnet 21. Quatrain 2 of Sonnet 21 even specifically
rejects a "proud compare" with the sun, exactly the comparison-
and-contrast dominating quatrain 2 of Sonnet 18. Sonnet 21's
"And then, believe me, my love is as fair / As any mother's child"
links it closely with Shakespeare's most famous sonnet on comparison, which again invokes the sun: Sonnet 130, "My mistress'
eyes are nothing like the sun," whose closing line, "As any she
belied with false compare," echoes both the affirming comparison
in 21.11–12 and the "proud compare" in 21.5.

These patterns, linking either almost adjacent sonnets or sonnets separated by over a hundred others, sonnets in the same sub-
sequence or in contrasting countersequences, amplify the resonance of the sonnets read in isolation. Yet Shakespeare also
ensures that *some* sonnets, like Sonnet 18, can be read on their
own, because the kind of effort needed to discover the more dis-
persed patterns linking sonnet and sonnet will be more than
some readers will be prepared to make.

For such readers, naturally in the majority, the immediate impact of stand-alone sonnets like 18 must suffice—and needs to be
intense enough to ensure that the sonnets as a whole remain in
high esteem, even if many readers know their range only by their
solitary peaks. Shakespeare certainly packs enough patterns even

into an uncomplicated and accessible sonnet like 18 to lure *some* readers further. The rhythms of day, season, and lifetime are familiar to us all but freshly felt in images like "Rough winds do shake the darling buds of May" or "Sometime too hot the eye of heaven shines." The tight quatrains mark their contours with internal repetition: in quatrain 1, *summer's . . . summers,* in quatrain 2, *Sometime . . . sometime* (with its glint or shadow, here, of *summertime*), in quatrain 3, *eternal . . . eternal.* The Petrarchan structure of octave and sestet, as often in the sonnets, complicates the Shakespearean quatrains-and-couplet structure, with the *volta* syntactically signaled at *"But* thy eternal summer shall not fade." That line, opening the sestet, replies at once to the "summer . . . sometime" repetition that binds the octave, as "that fair thou ow'st" in the next line responds to "every fair from fair sometime declines" in the octave. The pattern of repetition in the quatrains continues even into the brief couplet, with its "So long . . . So long." The triumphant final line clinches its force not just by sentiment but by pattern, with its repetition of stressed "this," its echo of "lives" in the *sound* of "gives" and the *sense* of "life," and with "*th*ee" alliterating with the double "*th*is."

Here as elsewhere, though, the most important patterns, for most readers, will be the emotions, in this case the tenderness and pride of the Poet's tribute and promise. These above all make the sonnet stand so well alone—and make it seem, in anthological isolation, to be addressed to a woman, or to anyone so beloved that one wishes to offer them the gift of a kind of immortality. Should the impact of that emotion move readers enough for them to search beyond the solo sonnet to its context, they can then discover other patterns of resonances, in the sonnet's role within the Poet's love for the Fair Youth, and in all the patterned artistry with which Shakespeare surrounds *this* sonnet's patterns, in its immediate contexts or over a hundred sonnets distant.

"A Lover's Complaint"

As a sonnet sequence the 1609 *Shake-speares Sonnets* has many
bibliographic peculiarities, among them the absence of a woman's
name in the title of the volume, the presence of the author's name
on the running heads on every page, and the inclusion of a separate poem, a narrative poem, "A Lover's Complaint," also attrib-
uted to Shakespeare, with its own title page, after the sonnets.
The peculiarity in this last case is not the presence of the narrative poem after a long sonnet sequence—a convention that amplified many of the most ambitious late Elizabethan sonnet
sequences—but the separate title page.

For many years "A Lover's Complaint" was presumed not to
be Shakespeare's, despite the title-page attribution: false title-
page attributions to Shakespeare (as to other successful authors)
were not an uncommon marketing ploy at the time. But in
1965 Kenneth Muir and MacDonald P. Jackson independently
reattributed "A Lover's Complaint" to Shakespeare,[24] and now
most editors of the *Sonnets* accept it as his,[25] especially after the
rediscovery of the sonnets-plus-verse-narrative pattern in the
sonnet sequences of other poets of Shakespeare's time, like Samuel Daniel, Thomas Lodge, Edmund Spenser, Giles Fletcher,
and Richard Barnfield.[26] Since this book focuses on lyrics, "A
Lover's Complaint," though part of the volume in which Shakespeare published *Shake-speares Sonnets,* might seem irrelevant—
but for two things.

First, the poem tells the story of a maid who resists a persistent
young man, who has proved irresistible to other young women.
The heroine knows of his reputation, and therefore doubles her
own resistance. This only encourages the man to persist all the
more, persuading her with promises of his unique adoration for her.
After overcoming her resistance, he blithely leaves her to repent in

the utmost distress. "A Lover's Complaint" tells the story, in other words, of a young woman who succumbs to a young man with the exceptional charms of the Fair Youth of the sonnets, beloved by all, but who, far from himself resisting women, persists even with the most resistant of women.

Second, after 152 poems in which he explores the resources of lyric,[27] Shakespeare now offsets these lyrics against a narrative—a narrative highly unlike that of his dramatic storytelling, but even more unlike the reflective voice of the Poet-speaker in the sonnets. In "A Lover's Complaint" Shakespeare works to the utmost the contrast with the sonnets' lyric mode: instead of speaking for himself, the Poet tells a story through the eyes of a bystander, to whom the young woman explains her distress by recounting the seductive words of the young man. Shakespeare's vivid, highly particularized visual description in "A Lover's Complaint," stylistically most unusual for him, evokes the heroine's world, far from the sophisticated milieu implied in the sonnets, to create a kind of hyperreal rural moral tableau.

The linear narrative of "A Lover's Complaint," scenic, pictorial, rural, moralized, archaized in diction and versification, indirect (via the old man's role as witness), dramatic (through the young woman's report) and multitiered (through the poet's report of the old man's hearing the young woman's report of the seducer's passionate but false protestations), contrasts on every dimension with the sonnets, at once intimate, almost overheard, thoughtscapes *and* artifacts consciously crafted for both immediate and perhaps real addressees in the poet's here and now and real but unknown and perhaps remote readers.

The emphatic difference of before and after for the young woman of "A Lover's Complaint"—all innocence and hope before, all self-reproach and despair after—contrasts emphatically with the sonnets. There, there seems neither before nor after, no sense of the sudden joy of falling in love, which Shakespeare can evoke so memorably and variously in his plays, but instead only love as an already achieved state. "Make thee another self for love of me" (10) and "O that you were yourself; but, love, you are / No longer yours than you yourself here live" (13) imply a steady feeling, rather than announcing a sudden qualitative change, just as "my mistress' eyes" (127) introduces the Poet's relationship with the Mistress as established fact rather than novel phase. Shakespeare provides no indication which relationship, his love for the Fair Youth or for the Mistress, began earlier. He merely requires that both relationships be already active when Youth and Mistress meet and feel a mutual attraction or more, so that their reciprocal feeling constitutes a betrayal of the Poet's love and friendship. But despite apparent betrayals on both sides, at various points in the sequence, the Poet addresses the Youth in the last of the sonnets to him as "O thou my lovely boy" (126). And although he *may* have had a view of his Mistress as "as rare / As any she belied with false compare" (130), but subsequently comes to view her with abhorrence, if also still with desire, he still defines his relation to her as love even in his last sonnet to her: "In loving thee thou know'st I am forsworn" (152). He may say, in this poem and earlier (147), "For I have sworn thee fair," but he has never done so in *these* poems. In the first of the Mistress sonnets, he calls her beautiful, in contrast to false would-be beauties, but two sonnets later he already talks of the aftermath of lust as "this hell" (129). The Mistress sonnets present no story of discovering disenchantment, but merely disclose the state of knowing it. Most emphatically of all, in the first sonnets to the Fair Youth, the Poet warns about the dangers of time and death, however fair he may be now—exactly as he does, over a hundred sonnets later, in the last of these sonnets to the Youth, Sonnet 126.

Long-Term and Short

In his sonnets to the Young Man, Shakespeare repeatedly affirms the immortality of his verse, in ways so eloquent that indeed they show no sign of dying. Achievement like this, like all "immortal" or at least lasting art, allows us to feel we cheat death in another way than the purely biological route of leaving offspring: it allows us to match thoughts and feelings across space and time, to connect with Shakespeare and his readers over centuries, to feel we are part of a human world of creation and communion that persists beyond our individual deaths.

Since Shakespeare so often affirms the immortality of his art, such immortality presumably mattered a good deal to him. In biological terms, this may seem odd. Evolution has bred in us emotions as motivations to act in ways that on average serve our ultimate advantage, our reproductive success. We strive, for instance, for status gains, and we dread status losses, because higher status, better access to resources, can make a difference to our survival and reproduction. Status beyond our lifetime, too, can make a difference to the access to resources available to our descendants and therefore, in biological terms, to our own ultimate fitness, since our genes endure in them. For that reason high social rank is hereditary among many primates, not just humans, and jealously hoarded, where possible, by those who have it.

But making intense efforts to secure an "immortal" status, a still longer-term fame, might seem in biological terms a cost without benefit. We could perhaps compare it to the follow-through in a golf swing or a tennis stroke. Although what happens to club or racquet after the ball leaves it can no longer affect the ball's flight, those previously committed to the follow-through will be more likely to send their balls farther and straighter. In the same way, perhaps, those committed to the long-term follow-through in time, to works attracting attention down the ages, commit more to the imaginative effort and therefore often secure better short-term results too.

Even apart from this, the motivation for "immortal" status makes sound human sense in the light of Terror Management Theory and the disturbing impact of our human consciousness of death. Individuals and communities haunted by imagining the finality of death—and this seems to be almost all of us—can feel that artists' works and the emotions they can evoke in us, including the feeling of respect or awe for their makers, can last beyond death. This sense that we belong to a creative and moral community whose values and best works can connect us with others past and to come can make a real difference to our motivation in the here and now.

Horace and Ovid wrote memorably of the immortality of art in terms that Shakespeare himself echoes, but no one before the Shakespeare of the sonnets had written so much or so eloquently on this theme. Without diminishing his express confidence in the immortality of his work, Shakespeare avoids the boastfulness of Horace, and therefore the likely resistance of readers to such insistence, by displacing the immortality onto the subject of the poems rather than their author. In appearing to offer immortality only to the "you" he never names, he also offers it in a sense to us, as well as himself, in the prospect that there are at least some thoughts and feelings and individuals who in some senses can last beyond death.

Shakespeare surely *sought* the immortal status he proclaimed for his verse, a longevity that could outlast even the Ovid, Seneca, and Plautus to whom he had been compared before he was halfway to the proverbial three-score-and-ten. But at the same time he seems to have been moved also by the much simpler drive for immediate status, particularly strong in males because of the force of sexual selection. Men with higher resources to offer appeal considerably more to women (and therefore leave more copies of themselves); most men, on the other hand, tend not to be especially attracted to women who have higher resources. Shakespeare chose to enter the field for the most intensely fought literary tournament of his day, the sonnet sequence. He seems to have sought to earn unusual attention by overturning sonnet conventions in the Mistress poems, only to have found that they undermined their own rationale and stopped the sequence short. By the time he found another way of challenging sonnet conventions more productively, in the Fair Youth poems, the sonnet-sequence wave had already passed its peak of popularity—if not yet of achievement.

Shakespeare ultimately composed a sonnet sequence that conformed to the outward local conventions—a two-part structure, a sonnet segue into narrative (153–154), a nonsonnet narrative afterpiece—yet outdid all other English sonneteers not only in the originality of his stratagems but simply in sheer number (and, as Paterson notes, in these "wildly competitive affairs . . . [a] poet would be judged on more than the length of his sequence, of course, but size counted for something").[28] In some senses, he might have done better to choose the best of his sonnets—the top ten, twenty, thirty, forty, perhaps even fifty?—to present nothing but clear successes. But that would have left Sidney, at 108 sonnets, seeming more fertile on at least one count. Shakespeare's competitiveness, we may well suspect, would not allow it. He may also have recognized that although most of his sonnets look far short of perfect by comparison with his own best, even they have an internal complexity that makes them at least as rich as the better sonnets of a Sidney or a Spenser. The very best of his sonnets, on the other hand—those most fondly remembered by those who read the sonnets today—were enough to earn the collection the immortality he confidently predicted.

In one sense, the sheer number of Shakespeare's sonnets seems to reflect an almost comical male competitiveness—a subject he even addresses in the Rival Poet section.[29] In another, it serves richer goals. By including *all* the sonnets he had written, apart from those embedded in his plays, he could maximize the openness of the lyric so central to the achievement of his sequence. The sheer number, the range of their moods and attitudes, the unpredictability in method and matter even within the strict structures of the sonnet, the range of possible kinds of patterns, even the sonnets' variability in quality, makes for a difference in reading experience as wide as possible from our engrossment in the developing narrative expectations of a story. Shakespeare would no doubt have preferred all his sonnets to be at the level of stand-alone tours de force, sonnets like 30, 60, 73, or 116, but even he could not accomplish that. But by the sheer number and range of his sonnets, he was able to show how deeply and widely he could explore the uniquely open possibilities that lyric verse can have in the absence of stories.

Envoi

Verse and Aversion

As we saw at the end of Chapter 7, a line like "And tongues-to-be your being shall rehearse" (81.11) demands a good deal even of native speakers of English, and would have done so already in Shakespeare's day—one reason perhaps why *Shake-speares Sonnets* as a volume seems not to have been successful for its first two centuries. Especially for readers unused to the conventions of poetry, a succession of lines like this (or "By oft predict that I in heaven find" [14.8] or "Mine eye my heart thy picture's sight would bar" [46.3]), requiring high concentration, can be too high a cost to pay.[1] Of course the expertise that comes with reading swathes of verse lowers the cost for those who particularly value its rewards, but even many lovers of poetry have over the years recoiled from the intricacies of Shakespeare's sonnets as a whole—although other enthusiastic readers have made it the most-loved verse collection of all.

The opportunities and the demands of the verse line, and the singular focus of attention it invites by working within the constraints of working memory, has had two consequences for verse. It has often become overloaded with novelty, or, alternatively, subject to conventions for exploiting the constraints of the line that have made an initial freshness, an attention-catching divergence from normal expectations, pall into routine. Poets resisting the conventions and the overchargedness of the verse line have often sought to cleanse and revitalize it, as William Carlos Williams famously did in "The Red Wheelbarrow" (1923):

so much depends
upon

a red wheel
barrow

glazed with rain
water

beside the white
chickens.[2]

Williams's lyric may seem as far removed as possible from Shakespeare's charged compression, but it, too, aims at seizing readers' attention through the unit of the verse line. It shocks those used to poetese, to the crowding of the line with pattern and distortions for pattern's sake. It appeals to naked perceptions, it makes the most of our customary expectation of more in a line or a poem by inviting us to pause at each line end, in a moment like a musical rest, while we linger over the words and the particular perceptions they activate in our imaginations. The poem resists our usual expectations of pattern and significance and, through the control of attention in the line, invites us to dwell on these concrete particulars, to *see* the particulars in our mind's eye and to reflect on them and on our seeing them. Exploiting the invitation to resonance in the lyric, Williams implicitly asks us to hold on to particular moments and perceptions, and to recognize the power of a poem to prompt us to share these perceptions, at least in imagination (the red wheelbarrow may have been no more visible to Williams than the Fair Youth to William S), and to share our sense of the value of holding on to perceptions, in face of the fleetingness of every moment, of all experience.

Whether surcharged with pattern, like Shakespeare's sonnets, or stripped of almost all pattern but perception and implicit emotion, like Williams's iconic lyric or a Basho haiku, poems address working memory one line-burst at a time. Most people find this delightful in the mid-range, from cradle song to love song, especially when coupled with the play of verbal pattern that we instinctively enjoy, and with the sense of control that verse lines and their patterned play can give, from Humpty Dumpty's sad end, through songs of romantic heartbreak, to condolence verse or funeral dirge. But who can wonder that many unused to ambitious verse find it taxing when poets' competition for attention weighs down the line or, in reply, makes it seem too light to catch? Much of poetic enjoyment comes naturally to us, but high poetic art often asks rather more, even as it promises more in return.

Even many lovers of literature resist high literary verse. The psychologist of art Colin Martindale has prophesied that verse will drive itself to extinction.[3] He argues that because all neural tissue responds less intensely when habituated—because creatures attend less, that is, to a repeated stimulus—poets seeking the attention of audiences will need to seek novelty at an ever more intense rate, to the point where serious verse will become incomprehensible. He tabulates objective measures of verbal novelty or strangeness through several centuries of European high literary verse, and thinks it confirms his prophesy.

Much in high literary verse does make it a minority taste: the absence of stories, in lyrics, or the presence of more efficient ways of making stories memorable than were possible for Homer or Virgil or Dante; the divergence from ordinary language, to make the most of the line as a unit of attention, and the tendency for such divergences to become routines, as in the Edwardian conventions that Modernist poets rebelled against, or the Modernist conventions that more recent poets rebel against, or the continuing tendency to become still more divergent from expectations; the tendency for lyrics to become self-contained puzzles, in their effort to appeal through the maximum concentration of language and pattern, and therefore to become more taxing than many readers will welcome.

Nevertheless, Martindale's prophesy is wrong.[4] Poets need not seek novelty on every measure simultaneously, only on some. Poets can also balance costs and benefits for their readers as well as for themselves. They can earn the attention of readers by reducing costs, by making their verse more accessible, as well as by raising benefits. If T. S. Eliot or Ezra Pound sought to refresh attention by rejecting old conventions and adding new benefits through a structure of mosaic allusiveness, Robert Frost could earn it by simplifying situations and expanding resonances, as in "Neither Out Far Nor in Deep."

I have noted the role that sexual selection may have played in Shakespeare's verse, albeit a minor role compared with much more general social selection—in the case of poetry, the simple but humanly profound desire to create what others will find worth their attention. But males are much more strongly sexually selected than females in most species, or, to rephrase, females are on average much more discriminating than males about whom they will partner. Males therefore have a more urgent need than females to prove themselves (except—and these exceptions prove the rule—in species in which the males invest more than the females in parental care). Some readers may resist what they wrongly suppose to be the implication that *I* suppose that males drive human creativity. Although at the level of public achievement this has often been true in the past, it has probably also been true even before female liberation that creativity at the private level has been driven as much by women as by men, as mate-choosers (preferring a subtle Odysseus to a boorish Antinous) and as child-raisers (telling fairy stories if not epics, inventing and singing lullabies, engaging in inventive interactive play).

Moreover in our species, males' presence during the uniquely long childhood their offspring face raises on average the offspring's chances of survival. This means that in our species not only do males need to compete for the scarce resources of, ultimately, females' egg-producing capacity, but females also need to compete for the scarce resources of male support, for the males with high current or likely future resources and the commitment to place what they have, or can earn, at the disposal of partners and children.[5] Males are swiftly attracted by physical beauty and youth, and women therefore compete with one another on these grounds; but both sexes are also attracted to intelligence, kindness, and creativity. As the work of Sarah Blaffer Hrdy in particular has shown, female primates, and especially women, have all along had to be active and creative strategizers precisely because of their role as primary caregivers.[6] Males have therefore selected long-term female partners on the basis of intelligence and kindness.

Although there are slight average differences on different brain tasks, there seem to be no differences between average male and female human intelligence. As a consequence of their social and technological release from domestic enslavement, women in many countries over the last century have been able to contribute more to public creativity and will have a still larger role to play the more widely they gain their freedom.

Anne Hathaway appears to have inspired the earliest of Shakespeare's surviving works, Sonnet 145, in what seems a classic, and successful, example of sexual selection: his creative intelligence at eighteen appealed enough to her, at twenty-six, for her to accept his advances. At that age, she had presumably resisted many suitors before she was charmed by someone whose intelligence augured well for the resources he was indeed able to secure as, eventually, the most successful writer of his time. Yet all she got out of the relationship, so the story goes, apart from the three children they shared, was the second-best bed he left her in his will.

I have described artists as active problem-solvers, aiming to earn attention for their work, intuitively assessing composition costs and benefits for themselves and comprehension costs and benefits for their readers. Carol Ann Duffy in the late 1990s, four centuries after Shakespeare, was already a prominent poet, was even proposed as British poet laureate, but was turned down, apparently, on the grounds of her lesbianism (she became poet laureate ten years later, in 2009). She chose to earn attention, and earned it, not by compounding the difficulty of modern high verse but by seeking out a new verbal accessibility, yet also new registers of verse language, especially by speaking as if through the mouths of others, and especially through including the excluded, like a murderously jealous boyfriend ("She used to meet some prick after work," in "Human Interest"). Famous for the evident feminism of her work, and for her poetic personas, she chose to make the most of her reputation and her convictions in *The World's Wife* (1999), a volume of poems in which she recasts history by speaking as if in the voices of those sidelined or overlooked by the male focus of most received history. Among the women whom she chose to speak through was Anne Hathaway. What would a feminist and a lesbian make of her?

ANNE HATHAWAY

"Item I gyve unto my wief my second best bed . . ."
(from Shakespeare's will)

The bed we loved in was a spinning world
of forests, castles, torchlight, clifftops, seas
where he would dive for pearls. My lover's words
were shooting stars which fell to earth as kisses
on these lips; my body now a softer rhyme
to his, now echo, assonance; his touch
a verb dancing in the centre of a noun.
Some nights, I dreamed he'd written me, the bed
a page beneath his writer's hands. Romance
and drama played by touch, by scent, by taste.
In the other bed, the best, our guests dozed on,
dribbling their prose. My living laughing love—
I hold him in the casket of my widow's head
as he held me upon that next best bed.

In the terms I have been using, Duffy brilliantly solves many problems at once. Like the problem of earning attention, especially by surprising expectations: by surprising our expectations of what someone of her reputation might write, like a reproach for Shakespeare's neglect of Anne Hathaway. (And he could indeed have neglected her: we simply do not know.) No: instead, by surprising our expectations, from the famous "second-best bed" and the Mistress in the sonnets, of Anne Hathaway's secondariness to Shakespeare. Duffy turns Anne into someone Will loves with all the heart and the imagination he put into his work. Far from being disregarded, *this* Anne expresses only her profound happiness in the man *she* sexually selected for his creativity, and herself shows a creativity and playfulness in reply in her lovemaking and her exuberant memories of their love. The exuberance of the poem invites the implication that Anne's creativity may have been what made Will persist in pursuing one so much older than would normally attract an eighteen-year-old's ardor.

Or the problem of finding a form. Duffy picks the sonnet, almost Shakespeare's only lyric mode outside the songs in his plays. By avoiding rhyme in the first twelve lines, she avoids the inversions that have become distasteful in modern poetry, but she wryly echoes, with a closing move to rhyme, the surprise of the change to the couplet that makes Shakespeare's sonnets so distinctive. Her rhyme ends on that "next best bed" but reaches it by the metaphor, so comic and tender at once, "I hold him in the casket of my widow's head." Duffy appeals to the lover of high literature by the allusiveness of her first two lines, but to all ready to enjoy a poem by the accessibility of the whole. And just as Shakespeare showed his competitiveness toward the sonneteers of his day, she relishes taking on the competition of the biggest literary word-slinger of them all, on his own territory, the sonnet as a love poem, and comes off—not second best.[7]

As long as lyrics can offer so much, they look like lasting.

Notes

Bibliography

Index

Notes

Introduction

1. Exceptions like Vikram Seth's 1986 novel in verse *The Golden Gate* or Sally Potter's 2004 iambic-pentameter movie *Yes* are almost vanishingly rare.
2. See Boyd, Carroll, and Gottschall 2010 for a selection and bibliography of work on literature and evolution. For more recent work, see the *Evolutionary Review* and Carroll 2011; Swirski 2010; Vermeule 2010. See Zunshine 2010 for recent cognitive literary studies.
3. Holmes 2010.
4. Paterson 2010: 14.

1. Poetry, Pattern, and Attention

1. Carey 2009.
2. Damasio 2000: 221.
3. Eimas 1997.

4. Boyd 2009b.

5. Pinker 1997; Scalise Sugiyama 2001, 2005; Tooby and Cosmides 2001; Carroll 2004, 2011.

6. Dissanayake 2000; Miall and Dissanayake 2003.

7. Trevarthen 1979; Pinker 1994.

8. Visual art: Kohn and Mithen 1999; music: Brown 2000; mime: Tomasello 2008.

9. M. Jackson 1982.

10. Anthropologist Donald E. Brown, characterizing the common features of the "Universal People," notes that "The UP . . . have poetry in which lines, demarcated by pauses, are about 3 seconds in duration. The poetic lines are characterized by the repetition of some structural, semantic, or auditory elements but by free variation too"; in Boyd, Carroll and Gottschall 2010: 85.

11. Dennett 1993: 184–186.

12. Pöppel 1988; Turner and Pöppel 1988.

13. Hogan 2003.

14. Brooks and Warren 1976.

15. Tomasello 1995.

16. Tomasello et al. 2005.

17. Doidge 2007.

18. Tsur 1998.

19. Fauconnier and Turner 2002.

20. Lea et al. 2008.

21. Scodel 2002.

22. Vanderbeke 2010.

23. Goleman 2006.

24. Vendler 1994: 37: "when I turned away from the oral model and read the poems on the quarto page . . . I saw things that uttering the sonnets as my own speech had not revealed. What I noticed on the page, especially in reading the quarto version of the *Sonnets,* were the many meaningful repetitions of identical or nearly identical words, syllables, and even letters."

25. Paterson 2010: 176: "If anyone ever tells you line-beginnings are as important as line-endings, ignore them. They aren't. The silent pause indicated by the right-hand margin means that whatever comes immediately before it will reverberate in its empty acoustic—the ear will simply hear those words more clearly; and in its composition, the poem will naturally distribute its semantic weight to take advantage of that pattern of end-silences."

26. Berlyne 1971, 1974; Martindale 1990.

27. See Hurley, Dennett, and Adams 2011 for a subtle analysis of unconscious expectation in humor in particular and cognition in general.

28. In "farfetched" I echo a fetching defense of rhyme by one of the best of modern rhymers, Richard Wilbur: "it is precisely in its power to suggest comparisons and connections—unusual ones—to the poet that one of the incidental merits of rhyme may be said to lie. Say to yourself *lake, rake,* and then write down all the metaphors and other reconciliations of these terms which occur to you within one or two minutes. It is likely to be a long list, extending from visual images of wind furrowing the water, to punning reminiscences of Lancelot and Guinevere. . . . the suggestions of rhyme are so nimble and so many that it is an invaluable means to the discovery of poetic raw material which is, in the very best sense, farfetched"; Wilbur 1976: 222–223.

29. Boyd 2009a.

30. Longenbach 2004.

2. Lyric and Sonnet

1. Lindley 1985; see also Brewster 2009.

2. Dickinson 1999: no. 1219.

3. See for instance Cánovas 2011 for an analysis of lyric micronarratives.

4. Sperber and Wilson 1988.

5. An anonymous reviewer for Harvard University Press comments: "Frost's poem isn't a story? It seems pretty Story-like to me." The speaker stops his horse in snowy woods, and has miles to go before he sleeps: resonant, like all great lyrics, in Frost's hands, but in the terms of recent narratology, low in "narrativity," in storyworthiness.

6. Jonathan Culler has explored the universalizing tendency in reading lyric verse in many works, beginning with his 1975 *Structuralist Poetics*.

7. Paterson 2010: xv.

8. Matching my stress on problems and solutions, Paterson observes that Henry Howard, the Earl of Surrey, who established this form, found "a solution to the problem of trying to write a fourteen-line poem using only four rhymes in a rhyme-poor language"; Paterson 2010: 489.

3. A First Shakespeare Sonnet

1. Pfister and Gütch 2009: 9.

2. All quotations from Shakespeare's poems are from Burrow 2002.

3. Vendler 1997/1999: 11.

4. Tsur 1998 critiques the false impressionistic responses to patterns of sound. His experimental results suggest that what linguists call construal is a key: that we want to maximize the cooperative attitude that successful linguistic comprehension requires in order to extract most pleasure and sense.

5. For discussions of this phenomenon in the sonnets, see Booth 1977/2000: xi, xiv, xvii; Atkins 2007: 32; Paterson 2010: 172.

6. Konner 2010: 512.

7. Burrow notes that what he prints as "And with old woes new wail my dear time's waste" "could equally well be modernized as 'And with old woes' new wail (noun) my dear times waste (verb). . . . Equally possible is 'times" rather than 'time's' "; 2002: 440.

8. Burrow 2002: 440, n. to line 1.

9. MacDonald P. Jackson, in his reader's report on this book for Harvard University Press, July 2011.

10. Ibid.

11. In English we can say "He runs" or "He quickly runs," and "He runs fast," but not "*He fast runs."

12. de Grazia 2007: 67.

13. Perner 1991; Sperber 2000; Saxe and Baron-Cohen 2007.

14. Dunbar 1996.

15. Goleman 2006.

16. Peskin 2010.

17. Another pattern I have just noticed, at the copyediting stage: the strange harmonies of lines 3 and line 8: "I sigh the lack of many a thing I sought . . . / And moan th' expense of many a vanished sight." The phrases "of many a thing I sought" and "of many a vanished sight" have the same first three words, the same rhythm, and the same consonants in the final word, with "sigh . . . sought" in line 3 as it were compacted into the "sought" of line 8. The "sigh . . . sought" sound-pairing also anticipates the "moan . . . many" in line 8. Apart from this sonnet's recurrent repetitions, conveyed especially through sonic patterning, I cannot see any particular point in this interplay of partial matches, but I can admire the extraordinary subtlety of the modulation.

18. Vendler 1997/1999.

19. I take the idea of understanding actions or effects through understanding the actor's "problem situation" from Karl Popper, 1974/1992: 134.

20. See Chapter 4 n.31 for a discussion of "problem situations."

4. Love: The Mistress

1. MacD. Jackson 2002b: 22.

2. MacD. Jackson 1965, 9b, 2000, 2001, 2002a, 2002b, 2005; Duncan-Jones 1983, 1997/2010; Edmondson and Wells 2004: 38.

3. Duncan-Jones 1997/2010; MacD. Jackson 1999a, 1999b, 2000, 2001, 2002a, 2002b; Burrow 2002.

4. Seabright 2012.

5. Pinker 2002: 407.

6. Only one woman poet published a sonnet sequence during the English sonnet vogue in the four decades from 1580, Lady Mary Wroth, in her *Pamphilia to Amphilanthus* (1621).

7. Boyd 2005.

8. Note that Benedick's sonnet is *to* Beatrice, even if their former display of mutual disdain has kept him too embarrassed to send it to her; Beatrice's seems a confession to herself rather than a sonnet *to* Benedick.

9. Gurr 1971; MacD. Jackson 2000: 129–130.

10. To look ahead to effects within the finished collection, many years later: MacD. Jackson 1999a and 2000: 129–131 shows how this sonnet, seemingly out of place between the psychologically powerful 144 and the religiously powerful 146, has had a niche crafted for it by the sustained rhyme-links running through the Mistress sonnets, and the fiend-heaven-hell image tying it by playful contrast with the serious sonnets fore and aft.

11. Ridley 2010.

12. J. Harris 2006.

13. See Sidanius and Pratto 1999 for massive empirical documentation.

14. D. Campbell 1960; Plotkin 1994; Simonton 1999.

15. Darwin 1871/2003: 112.

16. See, for instance, on empathy: Baron-Cohen 2003, 2011; de Waal 2009; on attunement: Goleman 2006; on joint attention: Tomasello 1995; Tomasello et al. 2005; on Theory of Mind: Saxe and Baron-Cohen 2007.

17. Seabright 2012, ch. 1.

18. See Trivers 1972 for the foundational analysis of male versus female parental investment in offspring.

19. Seabright 2012, ch. 1.

20. Hogan 2003.

21. Boyd 2009b.

22. *Palladis Tamia, Wits Treasury,* 1598, reproduced in Schoenbaum 1975: 140. MacD. Jackson 2005: 233–234 shows that Shakespeare read Meres carefully.

23. Hieatt, Hieatt, and Prescott 1991; MacD. Jackson 1999, 2002a, 2005.

24. MacD. Jackson 2001: 60.

25. MacD. Jackson 2002a: 239, 1999a, 2000.

26. For the best evidence of Shakespeare's ordering even of the Mistress poems, see MacD. Jackson 1999b, 2000: 130–131. I adduce later more evidence that clinches the case for *Shakespeare's* being the one responsible for placing 127 first in the Mistress sequence.

27. "Of all the great writers, Shakespeare is by far the most adamantly opposed to cosmetics" (David Mikics, in Burt and Mikics 2010: 66).

28. If sonnets as seduction poems form part of what Darwin identified as sexual selection, so does female "painting," as Shakespeare often calls makeup. Because in humans female beauty is the quickest trigger of male desire, and because human females have to compete among themselves for what, with long child care, becomes the limited resource of the best, the most supportive and reliable, long-term partners, female beauty becomes a key arena of intrasexual competition in humans, unlike in most other species: see A. Campbell 2011 and Seabright 2012.

29. I adopt the common emendation of "brows" for the Quarto's "eyes" in line 10, which many suppose a printer's erroneous repetition of "eyes" in line 9. The emendation is all the more likely in view of the strikingly close echo of *Love's Labour's Lost:*

> O, if in black my lady's brows be decked,
> It mourns that painting and usurping hair
> Should ravish doters with a false aspect;
> And therefore is she born to make black fair.
> Her favour turns the fashion of the days,
> For native blood is counted painting now;
> And therefore red, that would avoid dispraise
> Paints itself black, to imitate her brow. (IV.3.256–263)

Jackson's evidence for dating the Mistress sonnets close to the 1594–95 date for *Love's Labour's Los,* increases the likelihood of "brows" in line 10, as does the sonic interlacement of "power . . . borrowed . . . bower . . . brows."

30. As were the eyes of Sidney's Stella (*Astrophil and Stella* 7), although Sidney does not return to Stella's "blackness" beyond this sonnet.

31. Edmondson and Wells 2004: 42.

32. A problem-solution model, developed by Karl Popper for the historical explanation of scientific discovery, by his friend Ernst Gombrich for discovery in the visual arts, and more recently by David Bordwell in film studies, allows us to reconstruct situations and probable intentions in rich and realistic ways (Popper 1974/1992; Gombrich 1950, 1960; Bordwell 1997). All three scholars argue against explanations in terms of the times, since these can offer no fine-grained causal account of why *this* individual made *this* intellectual or creative move (Popper 1994; Gombrich 1991; Bordwell and Carroll 1996). An explanation in terms of an individual's problem situation within a particular creative field, on the other hand, pays close heed to the causally relevant context. It considers individuals as problem-solvers within contexts unique to them, given their own talents, training, interests, given their prior individual repertoire of favored problems and solutions and their individual degrees of awareness of the problems and solutions that others in the field have recently faced and found. Bordwell notes the range of publicly available cinematic problems and solutions at any one time, and their different degree of availability within different locations, or to filmmakers with different training or inclinations (Bordwell 1997: 150). For Shakespeare, as the author of highly successful plays and narrative poems, and as someone who searched in unique ways for new problems within his chosen modes, the problems of writing sonnets and shaping them into a sequence were both similar to those of other poets of his time and richly different.

33. Melchiori 1976: 15, 198.

34. Paterson 2010.

35. See, e.g., Boyd 1995.

36. MacD. Jackson 2005.

37. Booth 1977/2000: 456–457.

38. Wells 2010.

39. Paterson 2010: 381, 292.

40. Simonton 1999.

5. Love and Time: The Youth

1. Hieatt, Hieatt, and Prescott 1991; MacD. Jackson 1999a, 2001, 2002a, 2002b.

2. MacD. Jackson 2000.

3. Booth 1977/2000: 136.

4. Neely 1978.

5. Jackson was surprised at my pointing out the echoes of *fair* and *beauty*, but later noted—to the surprise of both of us, neither of us having remembered this—that he himself had noted it in MacD. Jackson 2000: 122.

6. Jackson, who alerted me to the duplication also of *sweet*, notes that a search on the Literature Online database (http://lion.chadwyck.co.uk) shows conjunctions of *fair* (in all possible forms), *beauty* (in all forms), *heir*, *sweet*, and *eyes* within eighty words nowhere else in Shakespeare, including other sonnets, outside Sonnets 1 and 127 (personal communication). When we add also *bear/bore*, the unique matching of lexical choices in the first sonnets of the Youth and Mistress sub-sequences can only be read as very highly deliberate.

7. With one exception, 15: see later discussion.

8. MacD. Jackson 1999a, 2001.

9. The two candidates usually proposed as the likeliest originals of the Young Man are Henry Wriothesley, third Earl of Southampton (1573–1624), the dedicatee of *Venus and Adonis* and *The Rape of Lucrece*, and William Herbert, third Earl of Pembroke (1580–1630), later to become a renowned literary patron and the dedicatee of the posthumous Shakespeare Folio of 1623. The speculation that Shakespeare could have been commissioned by the family of one of these noblemen begins with John Dover Wilson (Dover Wilson 1966). Duncan-Jones 1997/2010: 55 and MacD. Jackson 2001: 73–75 show that dates and other evidence favor Herbert over Southampton, although Shakespeare could easily have created the Fair Youth by combining both, or more.

10. See Crosman 1990 for a subtle analysis of the implicit growth of love in the first seventeen sonnets (which underplays, nevertheless, the peculiar intensity of feeling present from the start). See also MacD. Jackson 2002b for a detailed analysis of the pronouns here and later.

11. MacD. Jackson 2000: 121 n. 30 notes that this poem "has been enlisted as evidence both that Shakespeare was gay and that he was not. On the one hand, it repudiates any sexual interest in the Fair Youth and distinguishes between 'thy love,' which the Poet desires, and 'thy love's use,' which is physical and which the Poet happily assigns to his Friend's encounters with women. Yet, on the other hand, an undercurrent of prurient interest in the Youth's body, detectable in the specific bawdy references, has seemed to some readers to run counter to the overt argument."

12. Only one of Shakespeare's sonnets, 146, could be called religious. As Duncan-Jones notes, "Although the exclusion of Petrarch's treatment of secular love as a route to religious transcendence characterizes many English responses to Petrarchanism, it is unusually marked in the case of Shakespeare"; 1997/2010: 48.

13. MacD. Jackson 2000: 121–122 details the emphatic variety of Sonnets 18–26, the first to follow the variations on the procreation theme.

14. Ibid.: 132: "The Poet labours to idealize the Friend and demonize the Woman—repository for a vein of Renaissance misogyny associated with fear of thraldom to the flesh—and to preserve a dichotomy between Good and Evil, Love and Lust. But the opposites stray from their separate confines and bid to mingle."

15. Neely 1978.

16. Paterson 2010: 14.

17. Ibid.: 199.

18. Dubrow 1996: 292.

19. MacD. Jackson 2000: 115.

20. Ibid.: 117.

21. Edmondson and Wells 2004: 126.

22. Wells 2010: 65.

23. Ibid.

24. Emmott 1997.

25. Paterson 2010: 379.

26. Atkins 2007: 15.

27. Booth 1977: 548.

28. Parks 2007.

29. Wells 2010: 67.

6. Status

1. Paterson 2010: 492.

2. The temptation to dishonest signaling on the part of the male, and the motivation for females to discriminate honest from dishonest signaling, have been the subject of a whole literature in biology: see, e.g., Dawkins 1976/1989, chap. 12; Zahavi and Zahavi 1997; Miller 2000.

3. Henrich and Gil-White 2001.

4. MacD. Jackson 2001: 69.

5. MacD. Jackson 2000: 120, 2002b: 27.

6. Vendler 1997: 148.

7. E. O. Wilson 1975/2000: 280–282; Clutton-Brock and Parker 1995: 211.

8. Chance and Larsen 1976.

9. Boehm 1999.

10. Dawkins 1976/1989; Frank 1988; de Waal and Tyack 2003.

11. Tooby and Cosmides 1996. Hence the sting of Sonnet 87, with its relentless codification of the gift of friendship in mercantile and legalistic terms: "Farewell, thou art too dear for my possessing, / And like enough thou know'st thy estimate."

12. Bayley 1974.

13. Neill 2004; Schalkwyk 2008.

14. Kerrigan 1986: 244.

15. Ibid.

16. Kerrigan 1986; Schalkwyk 2002; MacD. Jackson 2002.

17. Evans 2006: 165.

18. For a superb analysis of Sonnet 111, "O, for my sake do you with Fortune chide," as Shakespeare's touchy response to recent slights on his status, see MacD. Jackson 2005.

19. Levin 2003.

20. Headlam Wells 2005.

7. Death

1. As was noted first by Derek Traversi in 1938, the word "time" occurs fifty-four times in the Youth sonnets but not at all in the Mistress sonnets (Traversi 1938/1968). "Death" and cognates (*dead, die/dies/diest, dying*) occur forty-five times in the Youth sonnets but only seven times in the Mistress sonnets, four of these in Sonnet 146, which focuses on death but has nothing to do with the Mistress or any other female.

2. Mithen 2001: 29.

3. Perner 1991; Sperber 2000.

4. This does not mean that we should see religion, even in evolutionary and cognitive terms, as only an attempted solution to the problem of death consciousness. Some religions do not concern themselves greatly with the fate of the self after death, and there appears to be strong evidence that religion can solve problems of social cohesion in life (D. Wilson 2002). There is also ample evidence that other by-products of our social imaginations

also bias us toward religious belief (Atran 2002; Boyer 2001; Barrett 2004). This is a rich field of investigation not only for those in religious studies but also for evolutionary and cognitive anthropologists, biologists, psychologists, and even economists.

5. Solomon, Greenberg, and Pyszczynski 1998; Arndt and Solomon 2003; Solomon et al. 2004; Landau et al. 2007; Landau, Sullivan, and Solomon 2010; Burke et al. 2010.

6. MacD. Jackson (2000: 127) explains why Sonnet 81, seemingly anomalous within the Rival Poets sequence, has been appropriately placed, in terms of its diction, its rhyming, and its subject matter.

7. For accounts of the force of construal in linguistics, rich in evolutionary considerations, see Verhagen 2007.

8. Duncan-Jones 1997/2010: 85–86.

9. For interesting recent work on the psychology of uplift and elevation, see Haidt 2006; for the counterdominance impulse, see Boehm 1999 and Carroll et al. 2010.

10. Landau et al. 2007.

8. Lyric and Narrative

1. Wordsworth 2004: 137.

2. Schiffer 1999: 14.

3. MacD. Jackson 2005: 244–245.

4. Ibid.: 226.

5. Jackson compellingly demonstrates that the figure(s) of the Rival Poet(s), in sonnets written between 1598 and 1600, conflate(s) Marlowe, Chapman, and Jonson (ibid.).

6. Analogously, modern fiction often resorts to the convenient convention of first-person narrative, even first-person narrative in the present tense, accepting the convention so lazily that writers rarely seek to explain why the narrator tells the story at all, or to whom, or has the time or talent to do so. Vladimir Nabokov is an exception: he always situates and motivates a Hermann, a Fyodor, a Humbert, a Kinbote, a Van Veen. William Shakespeare always situates and motivates the person writing his sonnets: Will Shakespeare, poet and player, musing on and often reaching out to an absent beloved.

7. Wordsworth 1984: 356.

8. Furnivall 1877/1896: lxiii–lxiv.

9. Crosman 1990: 472.

10. Hollander 2001: xxvi.

11. "To my mind the fact that Shakespeare's name was 'Will' increases the likelihood that [Sonnet 135] has a real-life addressee"; Wells 2010: 49.

12. Crosman 1990: 485.

13. Ibid.: 473–474.

14. C. S. Lewis describes the relationship to the Youth as "so odd a story that we find a difficulty in regarding it as fiction"; quoted in ibid.: 470.

15. Jonathan Bate writes: "To my ear, the bitterness of tone in certain of the sonnets is incompatible with the idea that they are mere exercises. But it could equally well be argued that Shakespeare knew how to mimic bitterness in his plays"; 2008: 52.

16. C. L. Barber writes: "It has been suggested that the friend and mistress are fictions created in the process of an exercise in conventional sonneteering, but this notion has not stood up. . . . And much of what is expressed concerning the friend and the mistress is most definitely *not* conventional sonneteering"; 1960/1987: 16.

17. Hunter 1953: 152.

18. Ibid.: 155.

19. Ibid.

20. Sir Sidney Lee famously called the sonnets "literary exercises" in the New York version of his Shakespeare entry in the 1897 volume of the *Dictionary of National Biography,* although in the London edition a few months previously he had written that "Attempts have been made to represent [the sonnets] as purely literary exercises" but that "Shakespeare avows, in phraseology that is often cryptic, the experiences of his own heart." Bate, who summarizes Lee's vacillations, himself rejects the idea that the sonnets are "mere exercises"; 2008: 42, 52.

21. I elaborate here on Jackson's elaboration of Vendler 1997: 22, in MacD. Jackson 2000: 123–124 and 2002b: 24, 27.

22. MacD. Jackson 2000: 134.

23. Burrow 2002: 416.

24. Muir 1965/1973; MacD. Jackson 1965, 2008.

25. Brian Vickers 2007 has strenuously advocated John Davies of Hereford's authorship of "A Lover's Complaint," but Jackson's responses (2008a, 2008b) have been considered decisive: "in two articles he disproves Brian Vickers's attribution of the poem *A Lover's Complaint* to John Davies of Hereford" (Egan 2010: 358).

26. Duncan-Jones 1983; Kerrigan 1986; Duncan-Jones 1997/2010.

27. In segueing from lyric sonnets to a narrative coda via the two narrative sonnets 153 and 154, Shakespeare was also following the pattern of the sonnet-sequence volume in his time: see Duncan-Jones 1983; Larsen, in Spenser 1997.

28. Paterson 2010: xii–xiii.

29. MacD. Jackson 2005: 243.

Envoi

1. Paterson observes that "Poetry . . . says 'it'll be worth your while to read in to this.' . . . Difficulty is built into the system" (2010: xvi). He also notes the cost-benefit ratio for readers: "this is the sort of poem I have in mind when I talk about the ratio between investment and reward" (ibid.: 77).

2. Williams 1986: 224.

3. Martindale 1990, 2009.

4. Boyd 2009a.

5. A. Campbell 2011.

6. Hrdy 1999, 2009.

7. Just as Duffy will take Shakespeare on not as a sonneteer but as the composer of a love-series in her splendid *Rapture* (2005). Katherine Duncan-Jones, one of the foremost editors of Shakespeare's *Sonnets,* singles out, in a review of *The Art of the Sonnet* (Burt and Mikics 2010), Alison Brackenbury's "Homework. Write a Sonnet. About Love?" (2004), for "vigorously challeng[ing] the sonnet form and its traditional associations with male-voiced love" (2010: 10).

Bibliography

Editions of Shakespeare's *Sonnets* are listed under their editors or commentators, Booth, Burrow, Dover Wilson, Duncan-Jones, Evans, Kerrigan, Orgel, Paterson, Rollins, Vendler, West.

Abrams, M. H. 1988. *A Glossary of Literary Terms.* 5th ed. (1st ed., 1957.) New York: Harcourt Brace Jovanovich.

Allen, Michael J. B. 1979. "Shakespeare's Man Descending a Staircase: Sonnets 126 to 154." *Shakespeare Survey* 31: 127–138.

Alpers, Paul. 2002. "Learning from the New Criticism: The Example of Shakespeare's Sonnets." In *Renaissance Literature and Its Formal Engagements,* ed. Mark David Rasmussen. New York: Palgrave, 115–138.

Arndt, Jamie, and Sheldon Solomon. 2003. "The Control of Death and the Death of Control: The Effects of Mortality Salience, Neuroticism and Worldview Threat on the Desire for Control." *Journal of Research in Personality* 37: 1–22.

Atkins, Carl F., ed. 2007. *Shakespeare's Sonnets with Three Hundred Years of Commentary.* Madison, N.J.: Fairleigh Dickinson University Press.

Atran, Scott. 2002. *In Gods We Trust: The Evolutionary Landscape of Religion.* New York: Oxford University Press.

Barber, C. L. 1960/1987. "An Essay on Shakespeare's Sonnets." 1960. Reprinted in Harold Bloom, ed., *Shakespeare's Sonnets.* New York: Chelsea House, 1987, 5—27.

Barnfield, Richard. 1990. *The Complete Poems.* Ed. George Klawitter. Selinsgrove, Pa.: Susquehanna University Press.

Baron-Cohen, Simon. 2003. *The Essential Difference: Male and Female Brains and the Truth about Autism.* New York: Basic Books.

———. 2011. *The Science of Evil: On Empathy and the Origins of Human Cruelty.* New York: Basic Books.

Barrett, Justin L. 2004. *Why Would Anyone Believe in God?* Lanham, Md.: Altamira.

Bate, Jonathan. 2008. *The Genius of Shakespeare.* Oxford: Oxford University Press.

Bayley, John. 1974. "Who Was the 'man right fair' of the Sonnets?" *Times Literary Supplement,* January 4: 15.

Bell, Ilona. 2007. "Rethinking Shakespeare's Dark Lady." In Schoenfeldt, 293–313.

Berlyne, Daniel E. 1971. *Aesthetics and Psychobiology.* New York: Appleton-Century-Crofts.

———, ed. 1974. *Studies in the New Experimental Aesthetics: Steps toward an Objective Psychology of Aesthetic Appreciation.* Washington, D.C.: Hemisphere.

Boehm, Christopher. 1999. *Hierarchy in the Forest: The Evolution of Egalitarian Behavior.* Cambridge, Mass.: Harvard University Press.

Booth, Stephen, ed. 1977/2000. *Shakespeare's Sonnets.* New Haven, Conn.: Yale University Press.

———. 2007. "The Value of the Sonnets." In Schoenfeldt, 15–26.

Bordwell, David. 1997. *On the History of Film Style.* Cambridge, Mass.: Harvard University Press.

Bordwell, David, and Noël Carroll. 1996. *Post-Theory: Reconstructing Film Studies.* Madison: University of Wisconsin Press.

Boyd, Brian. 1995. "*King John* and *The Troublesome Raigne*: Sources, Structure, Sequence." *Philological Quarterly* 74: 37–56.

———. 2004. "Laughter and Literature: A Play Theory of Humor." *Philosophy and Literature*, 28: 1–22.

———. 2005. "Evolutionary Theories of Art." In Gottschall and Wilson, 149–178.

———. 2009a. "Art, Innovation and Attention." *Empirical Studies of the Arts* 27(2): 141–145.

———. 2009b. *On the Origin of Stories: Evolution, Cognition, and Fiction*. Belknap Press of Harvard University Press.

———. 2010a. Review of Indira Ghose, *Shakespeare and Laughter: A Cultural History*. *Review of English Studies*, n.s. 61(249): 301–303.

———. 2010b. "Why We Love Fiction." *Axess*, 2 October, http://www.axess.se/magasin/english.aspx?article=762.

———. 2011a. "Verse: Universal? Adaptive? Aversive?" *Evolutionary Review: Art, Culture, Science* 2: 86–96.

———, ed. 2011b. Vladimir Nabokov, *"Pale Fire: A Poem in Four Cantos" by John Shade*. Berkeley, Calif.: Gingko Press.

Boyd, Brian, Joseph Carroll, and Jonathan Gottschall, eds. 2010. *Evolution, Literature, and Film: A Reader*. New York: Columbia University Press.

Boyer, Pascal. 2001. *Religion Explained: The Evolutionary Origins of Religious Thought*. New York: Basic Books.

Brackenbury, Alison. 2004. *Bricks and Ballads*. Manchester: Carcanet Press.

Brewster, Scott. 2009. *Lyric*. London: Routledge.

Brooks, Cleanth, and Robert Penn Warren. 1976. *Understanding Poetry*. 4th ed. New York: Holt, Rinehart and Winston.

Brown, Steven. 2000. "The 'Musilanguage' Model of Music Evolution." In *The Origins of Music*, ed. Nils L. Wallin, Björn Merker, and Steven Brown. Cambridge, Mass.: Bradford/MIT Press, 271–300.

Burke, Brian L., Andy Martens, and Erik H. Faucher. 2010. "Two Decades of Terror Management Theory: A Meta-Analysis of Mortality Salience Research." *Personality and Social Psychology Review*. 14: 155–195.

Burrow, Colin, ed. 2002. William Shakespeare, *Complete Sonnets and Poems*. Oxford: Oxford University Press.

Burt, Stephen, and David Mikics. 2010. *The Art of the Sonnet*. Cambridge, Mass.: Belknap Press of Harvard University Press.

Callaghan, Dympna. 2007. *Shakespeare's Sonnets*. Oxford: Blackwell.

Campbell, Anne. 2011. "Ladies, Choose Your Weapons." *Evolutionary Review: Art, Science, Culture* 2: 106–112.

Campbell, Donald. 1960. "Blind Variation and Selective Retention in Creative Thought as in Other Knowledge Processes." *Psychological Review* 67: 380–400.

Cánovas, Cristóbal Pagán. 2011. "Erotic Emissions in Greek Poetry: A Generic Integration Network." *Cognitive Semiotics* 6.

Carey, Benedict. 2009. "How Nonsense Sharpens the Intellect." *New York Times,* October 5, http://www.nytimes.com/2009/10/06/health /06mind.html?scp=5&sq=%22benedict%20carey%22&st=cse.

Carlisle, Carol. 1979. "Shakespeare's Sonnet 127." *Explicator* 38: 33–35.

Carroll, Joseph. 2004. *Literary Darwinism: Evolution, Human Nature, and Literature.* New York: Routledge.

———. 2011. *Reading Human Nature: Literary Darwinism in Theory and Practice.* Albany: State University of New York Press.

Carroll, Joseph, Jonathan Gottschall, John Johnson, and Daniel Kruger. 2010. "Paleolithic Politics in British Novels of the Nineteenth century." In Boyd, Carroll, and Gottschall, 480–506.

Chance, M. R. A., and R. R. Larsen, eds. 1976. *The Social Structure of Attention.* London: John Wiley.

Clutton-Brock, T. H., and G. A. Parker. 1995. "Punishment in Animal Societies." *Nature* 373: 209–216.

Corish, Denis. 2000. " 'The world's due, by the grave and thee': Shakespeare, Sonnet 1.14." *Notes and Queries,* December: 453–55.

Crosman, Robert. 1990. "Making Love out of Nothing at All: The Issue of Story in Shakespeare's Procreation Sonnets." *Shakespeare Quarterly* 41: 470–488.

Culler, Jonathan. 1975. *Structuralist Poetics: Structuralism, Linguistics and the Study of Literature.* London: Routledge and Kegan Paul.

Damasio, Antonio. 2000. *The Feeling of What Happens: Body, Emotion, and the Making of Consciousness.* London: Vintage.

Daniel, Samuel. 1969. *Delia; with, The Complaint of Rosamond.* Menston: Scolar Press.

———. 1998. *Samuel Daniel: Selected Poetry and A Defense of Rhyme.* Ed. Geoffrey G. Hiller and Peter L. Groves. Asheville, N.C.: Pegasus Press.

Darwin, Charles. 1871/2003. *The Descent of Man and Selection in Relation to Sex.* London: Gibson Square Books.

Dawkins, Richard. 1976/1989. *The Selfish Gene*. 2d ed. Oxford: Oxford University Press.

de Grazia, Margreta. 2007. "Revolution in *Shake-speares Sonnets*." In Schoenfeldt, 57–69.

Deidda, Angelo. 2003. "The Metaphor of Increase and the Poetics of Decrease in Shakespeare's Sonnets." In *Una civile conversazione. Lo scambio letterario e culturale anglo-italiano nel Rinascimento/A Civil Conversation: Anglo-Italian Literary and Cultural Exchange in the Renaissance*, ed. K. Elam and F. Cioni. Bologna: Clueb, 225–234.

Dennett, Daniel C. 1993. *Consciousness Explained*. Harmondsworth: Penguin.

———. 1995. *Darwin's Dangerous Idea: Evolution and the Meanings of Life*. London: Penguin.

———. 2003. *Freedom Evolves*. New York: Viking.

de Waal, Frans. 1996. *Good Natured: The Origins of Right and Wrong in Humans and Other Animals*. Cambridge, Mass.: Harvard University Press.

———. 2009. *The Age of Empathy: Nature's Lessons for a Kinder Society*. New York: Harmony Books.

de Waal, Frans, and P. L. Tyack, eds. 2003. *Animal Social Complexity: Intelligence, Culture, and Individualized Societies*. Cambridge, Mass.: Harvard University Press.

Dickinson, Emily. 1999. *The Poems of Emily Dickinson: Reading Edition*. Ed. Ralph W. Franklin. Cambridge, Mass.: Harvard University Press.

Dissanayake, Ellen. 2000. *Art and Intimacy: How the Arts Began*. Seattle: University of Washington Press.

Djikic, Maja, Keith Oatley, Sara Zoeterman, and Jordan B. Peterson. 2009. "On Being Moved by Art: How Reading Fiction Transforms the Self." *Creativity Research Journal* 21: 24–29.

Doidge, Norman. 2007. *The Brain That Changes Itself: Stories of Personal Triumph from the Frontiers of Brain Science*. New York: Penguin.

Dolan, Neal. 2002. "Shylock in Love: Economic Metaphors in Shakespeare's Sonnets." *Raritan* 22 (Fall): 26–51.

Dover Wilson, John, ed. 1966. William Shakespeare, *The Sonnets*. Cambridge: Cambridge University Press.

Drayton, Michael. 1953. *Poems*. Ed. John Buxton. 2 vols. London: Routledge and Kegan Paul.

Dubrow, Heather. 1981. "Shakespeare's Undramatic Monologues: Toward a Reading of the *Sonnets*." *Shakespeare Quarterly*, 32(1): 1, 55–68.

———. 1996. "'Incertainties now crown themselves assur'd': The Politics of Plotting Shakespeare's Sonnets." *Shakespeare Quarterly* 47: 291–305.

———. 2007. "'Dressing old words new'? Re-evaluating the 'Delian Structure.'" In Schoenfeldt, 90–103.

Duffy, Carol Ann. 1985. *Standing Female Nude*. London: Anvil.

———. 1999. *The World's Wife*. London: Picador.

———. 2005. *Rapture*. London: Picador.

Dunbar, Robin. 1996. *Grooming, Gossip, and the Evolution of Language*. London: Faber.

Duncan-Jones, Katherine. 1983. "Was the 1609 *Shake-speare's Sonnets* Really Unauthorized?" *Review of English Studies* 34: 151–171.

———, ed. 1997/2010. *Shakespeare's Sonnets*. 2d ed. London: Methuen.

———. 2010. "Who Was Cynthia?" *Times Literary Supplement*, June 4: 10.

Dutton, Richard. 2007. "*Shake-speares Sonnets*, Shakespeare's Sonnets, and Shakespearean Biography." In Schoenfeldt, 121–136.

Eagleton, Terry. 2009. "Darwin Won't Help." *London Review of Books*, September 24.

Edmondson, Paul, and Stanley Wells. 2004. *Shakespeare's Sonnets*. Oxford: Oxford University Press.

Egan, Gabriel. 2010. "Shakespeare: Editorial and Textual Matters." *Year's Work in English Studies* 89: 337–364.

Eimas, P. D. 1997. "Infant Speech Perception: Processing Characteristics, Representational Units, and the Learning of Words." In *Perceptual Learning: The Psychology of Learning and Motivation*, ed. R. Goldstone. San Diego: Academic: 127–169.

Emmott, Catherine. 1997. *Narrative Comprehension: A Discourse Perspective*. Oxford: Clarendon Press.

Engle, Lars. 2007. "William Empson and the Sonnets." In Schoenfeldt, 163–182.

Evans, G. Blakemore, ed. 2006. William Shakespeare, *The Sonnets*. Cambridge: Cambridge University Press.

The Evolutionary Review: Art, Culture, Science. 2010–.

Fauconnier, Gilles, and Mark Turner. 2002. *The Way We Think: Conceptual Blending and the Mind's Hidden Complexities*. New York: Basic Books.

Frank, Robert. 1988. *Passions within Reason: The Strategic Role of the Emotions.* New York: Norton.

Furnivall, Frederick, ed. 1877/1896. *The Leopold Shakespeare.* London: Cassell.

Geary, David C. 2004. *The Origin of Mind: Evolution of Brain, Cognition, and General Intelligence.* Washington, D.C.: American Psychological Association.

Gervais, Matthew, and David Sloan Wilson. 2005. "The Evolution and Functions of Laughter and Humor: A Synthetic Approach." *Quarterly Review of Biology* 80: 395–430.

Goleman, Daniel. 2006. *Social Intelligence: The New Science of Human Relationships.* New York: Bantam.

Gombrich, Ernst. 1950. *The Story of Art.* London: Phaidon.

———. 1960. *Art and Illusion: A Study in the Psychology of Pictorial Representation.* London: Phaidon.

———. 1991. *Topics of Our Time: Twentieth-Century Issues in Learning and in Art.* London: Phaidon.

Gottschall, Jonathan. 2012. *The Storytelling Animal: How Stories Make Us Human.* New York: Harcourt Houghton Mifflin.

Gottschall, Jonathan, and David Sloan Wilson, eds. 2005. *The Literary Animal: Evolution and the Nature of Narrative.* Evanston, Ill.: Northwestern University Press.

Greenblatt, Stephen. 2004. *Will in the World: How Shakespeare Became Shakespeare.* New York: Norton.

Gurr, Andrew. 1971. "Shakespeare's First Poem: Sonnet 145." *Essays in Criticism* 21: 221–226.

Haidt, Jonathan. 2006. *The Happiness Hypothesis: Finding Modern Truth in Ancient Wisdom.* New York: Basic Books.

Harris, Judith Rich. 2006. *No Two Alike: Human Nature and Human Individuality.* New York: Norton.

Harris, Sam. 2010. *The Moral Landscape: How Science Can Determine Human Values.* London: Bantam.

Headlam Wells, Robin. 2005. *Shakespeare's Humanism.* Cambridge: Cambridge University Press.

Henrich, Joseph, and Francisco J. Gil-White. 2001. "The Evolution of Prestige: Freely Conferred Deference as a Mechanism for Enhancing the Benefits of Cultural Transmission." *Evolution and Human Behavior* 22: 165–196.

Hieatt, A. Kent, Charles W. Hieatt, and Anne Lake Prescott. 1991.
"When Did Shakespeare Write Sonnets 1609?" *Studies in Philology*
88(1): 69–109.

Hogan, Patrick Colm. 2003. *The Mind and Its Stories: Narrative
Universals and Human Emotion*. Cambridge: Cambridge University
Press.

Hollander, John. 2001. "Introduction." In Orgel.

Holmes, John. 2010. "Evolutionary Criticism and Epic Poetry: Brian
Boyd, On the Origin of Stories, Jonathan Gottschall, The Rape of
Troy, and Clinton Machann, Masculinity in Four Victorian Epics."
British Society for Literature and Science. http://www.bsls.ac.uk/
reviews/general-and-theory/evolutionary-criticism-and-epic-poetry
-brian-boyd-on-the-origin-of-stories-jonathan-gottschall-the-rape-of
-troy-and-clinton-machann-masculinity-in-four-victorian-epics/.

Hrdy, Sarah Blaffer. 1999. *Mother Nature: A History of Mothers, Infants,
and Natural Selection*. New York: Pantheon.

———. 2009. *Mothers and Others: The Evolutionary Origins of Mutual
Understanding*. Cambridge, Mass.: Belknap Press of Harvard University Press.

Hunter, G. K. 1953. "The Dramatic Technique of Shakespeare's Sonnets."
Essays in Criticism 3: 152–164.

Hurley, Matthew M., Daniel C. Dennett, and Reginald B. Adams Jr.
2011. *Inside Jokes: Using Humor to Reverse-Engineer the Mind*. Cambridge, Mass.: MIT Press.

Jablonka, Eva, and Marion J. Lamb. 2005. *Evolution in Four Dimensions:
Genetic, Epigenetic, Behavioral, and Symbolic Variation in the History of
Life*. Cambridge, Mass.: Bradford/MIT.

Jackson, MacDonald. P. 1965. *Shakespeare's "A Lover's Complaint": Its
Date and Authenticity*. Auckland: University of Auckland Bulletin 72,
English Series 13.

———. 1999a. "Rhymes in Shakespeare's *Sonnets*: Evidence of Date of
Composition." *Notes and Queries*, June: 213–219.

———. 1999b. "*Shakespeare's Sonnets*: Rhyme and Reason in the Dark
Lady Series." *Notes and Queries*, June: 219–222.

———. 2000. "Aspects of Organisation in *Shakespeare's Sonnets* (1609)."
Parergon 17: 109–134.

———. 2001. "Vocabulary and Chronology: The Case of Shakespeare's
Sonnets." *Review of English Studies*, n.s. 52: 59–75.

———. 2002a. "Dating Shakespeare's Sonnets: Some Old Evidence Revisited." *Notes and Queries,* June: 237–241.

———. 2002b. "The Distribution of Pronouns in *Shakespeare's Sonnets.*" *AUMLA* 97: 22–38.

———. 2005. "Francis Meres and the Cultural Contexts of Shakespeare's Rival Poet Sonnets." *Review of English Studies,* n.s. 56: 224–246.

———. 2008a. "The Authorship of *A Lover's Complaint:* A New Approach to the Problem." *PBSA* 102: 285–313.

———. 2008b. "*A Lover's Complaint, Cymbeline,* and the Shakespeare Canon: Interpreting Shared Vocabulary." *Modern Language Review* 103(3): 621–638.

Jackson, Michael. 1982. *Allegories of the Wilderness: Ethics and Ambiguity in Kuranko Narratives.* Bloomington: Indiana University Press.

Kennedy, X. J., Dana Gioia, and Mark Bauerlein. 2009. *Handbook of Literary Terms: Literature, Language, Theory.* 2d ed. New York: Pearson/Longman.

Kerrigan, John, ed. 1986. William Shakespeare, *The Sonnets and A Lover's Complaint.* London: Penguin.

Kiberd, Declan. 2009. *"Ulysses" and Us: The Art of Everyday Life in Joyce's Masterpiece.* New York: Norton.

Kohn, Marek, and Steven Mithen. 1999. "Handaxes: Products of Sexual Selection?" *Antiquity* 73: 518–526.

Konner, Melvin. 2010. *The Evolution of Childhood: Relationships, Emotion, Mind.* Cambridge, Mass.: Belknap Press of Harvard University Press.

Landau, Mark J., Sheldon Solomon, Tom Pyszczynski, and Jeff Greenberg. 2007. "On the Compatibility of Terror Management Theory and Perspectives on Human Evolution." *Evolutionary Psychology* 5: 476–519.

Landau, Mark J., Daniel Sullivan, and Sheldon Solomon. 2010. "On Graves and Graven Images: A Terror Management Analysis of the Psychological Functions of Art." *European Review of Social Psychology* 21: 114–154.

Lea, R. Brooke, David N. Rapp, Andrew Elfenbein, Aaron D. Mitchel, and Russell Swinburne Romine. 2008. "Sweet Silent Thought: Alliteration and Resonance in Poetry Comprehension." *Psychological Science* 19: 709–716.

Lee-Hamilton, Eugene. 2001. *The Selected Poems of Eugene Lee-Hamilton (1845–1907): A Victorian Craftsman Rediscovered.* Ed. MacDonald. P. Jackson. Lewiston, N.Y.: Edwin Mellen.

Levin, Richard. 2003. *Looking for an Argument: Critical Encounters with the New Approaches to the Criticism of Shakespeare and His Contemporaries.* Madison, N.J.: Fairleigh Dickinson University Press.

Lindley, David. 1985. *Lyric.* London: Methuen.

Longenbach, James. 2004. *The Resistance to Poetry.* Chicago: University of Chicago Press.

Mars-Jones, Adam. 2010. "Reading Shakespeare's Sonnets: A New Commentary by Don Paterson." *The Observer,* November 7.

Martindale, Colin. 1990. *The Clockwork Muse: The Predictability of Artistic Change.* New York: Basic Books.

——. 2009. "The Evolution and End of Art as Hegelian Tragedy." *Empirical Studies of the Arts,* 27(2): 133–140.

Melchiori, Giorgio. 1976. *Shakespeare's Dramatic Meditations: An Experiment in Criticism.* Oxford: Clarendon Press.

Miall, David S., and Ellen Dissanayake. 2003. "The Poetics of Babytalk." *Human Nature* 14: 337–364.

Miller, Geoffrey. 2000. *The Mating Mind: How Sexual Choice Shaped the Evolution of Human Nature.* New York: Doubleday.

Mithen, Steven. 2001. "The Evolution of Imagination: An Archaeological Perspective." *SubStance* 94/95: 28–54.

Muir, Kenneth. 1965/1973. "'A Lover's Complaint': A Reconsideration." Reprinted in Muir, *Shakespeare the Professional and Related Studies.* London: Heinemann, 1973, 204–219.

Neely, Carol Thomas. 1978. "The Structure of English Renaissance Sonnet Sequences." *ELH* 45(3): 359–389.

Neill, Michael. 2004. *Servile Ministers: Othello, King Lear and the Sacralization of Service.* Vancouver: Ronsdale Press.

Nordlund, Marcus. 2007. *Shakespeare and the Nature of Love: Literature, Culture, and Evolution.* Evanston, Ill.: Northwestern University Press.

North, Marcy L. 2007. "The *Sonnets* and Book History." In Schoenfeldt, 204–221.

Oatley, Keith. 2011. *Such Stuff as Dreams: The Psychology of Fiction.* Chichester: Wiley-Blackwell.

Orgel, Stephen, ed. 2001. William Shakespeare, *The Sonnets.* New York: Penguin.

——. 2007. "Mr. Who He?" In Schoenfeldt, 137–144.

Parks, Tim. "Veteran Straight Directors Whose Work Has Improved Gay Visibility (And Some Whose Hasn't)," June 24, 2007, http://www.afterelton.com/movies/2007/6/gayfriendlydirectors.

Paterson, Don, ed. 2010. *Reading Shakespeare's Sonnets: A New Commentary*. London: Faber and Faber.

Paul, Robert A. 2000. "Sons or Sonnets: Nature and Culture in a Shakespearean Anthropology." *Current Anthropology* 41(1): 1–9.

Perner, Josef. 1991. *Understanding the Representational Mind*. Cambridge, Mass.: MIT Press.

Peskin, Joan. 2010. "The Development of Poetic Literacy." *Discourse Processes* 47(2): 77–103.

Peskin, Joan, and David Olson. 2004. "On Reading Poetry: Expert and Novice Knowledge." In *Later Language Development: Typological and Psycholinguistic Perspectives,* ed. Ruth Berman. TiLAR (Trends in Language Acquisition) series, vol. 3. Amsterdam: John Benjamins, 211–232.

Petrarch. 1996. *The Canzoniere*. Trans. with commentary by Mark Musa. Bloomington: Indiana University Press.

Pfister, Manfred, and Jürgen Gütsch, eds. 2009. *William Shakespeare's Sonnets for the First Time Globally Reprinted: A Quatercentenary Anthology*. Dozwil: Signathur.

Pinker, Steven. 1994. *The Language Instinct*. New York: William Morrow.

———. 1997. *How the Mind Works*. New York: Norton.

———. 2002. *The Blank Slate: The Modern Denial of Human Nature*. New York: Penguin.

Plotkin, Henry. 1994. *Darwin Machines and the Nature of Knowledge*. Cambridge, Mass.: Harvard University Press.

Pöppel, Ernst. 1988. *Grenzen des Bewußtseins*. Stuttgart: Deutsche Verlags-Anstalt.

Popper, Karl. 1974/1992. *Unended Quest: An Intellectual Autobiography*. Rev. ed. London: Routledge.

———. 1994. *The Myth of the Framework: In Defence of Science and Rationality*. Ed. Mark Notturno. London: Routledge.

———. 1999. *All Life Is Problem-Solving*. Trans. P. Camiller. London: Routledge.

Radcliffe Richards, Janet. 2000. *Human Nature after Darwin: A Philosophical Introduction*. London: Routledge.

Richerson, Peter J., and Robert Boyd. 2005. *Not by Genes Alone: How Culture Transformed Human Evolution*. Chicago: University of Chicago Press.

Ridley, Matt. 2003. *Nature via Nurture: Genes, Experience, and What Makes Us Human*. New York: HarperCollins.

———. 2010. *The Rational Optimist: How Prosperity Evolves*. London: Fourth Estate.

Roche, Thomas P. 1989. *Petrarch and the English Sonnet Sequences*. New York: AMS Press.

Rollins, Hyder Edward, ed. 1944. *A New Variorum Edition of Shakespeare: The Sonnets*. 2 vols. Philadelphia: J. B. Lippincott.

Saxe, Rebecca, and Simon Baron-Cohen. 2007. *Theory of Mind*. Special issue of *Social Neuroscience*. Hove: Psychology Press.

Scalise Sugiyama, Michelle. 2001. "Narrative Theory and Function: Why Evolution Matters." *Philosophy and Literature* 25: 233–250.

———. 2005. "Reverse Engineering Narrative: Evidence of Special Design." In Gottschall and Wilson, 177–196.

Schalkwyk, David. 2002. *Speech and Performance in Shakespeare's Sonnets and Plays*. Cambridge: Cambridge University Press.

———. 2008. *Shakespeare, Love and Service*. Cambridge: Cambridge University Press.

Schiffer, James. 1999. "Reading New Life into Shakespeare's Sonnets: A Survey of Criticism." In *Shakespeare's Sonnets: Critical Essays*, ed. Schiffer. New York: Garland, 3—71.

———. 2007. "The Incomplete Narrative of Shakespeare's Sonnets." In Schoenfeldt, 45–56.

Schoenbaum, Samuel. 1975. *William Shakespeare: A Documentary Life*. New York: Oxford University Press.

Schoenfeldt, Michael, ed. 2007. *A Companion to Shakespeare's Sonnets*. Malden, Mass.: Blackwell.

Scodel, Ruth. 2002. *Listening to Homer: Tradition, Narrative, and Audience*. Ann Arbor: University of Michigan Press.

Seabright, Paul. 2004/2010. *The Company of Strangers: A Natural History of Economic Life*. Rev. ed. Princeton: Princeton University Press.

———. 2012. *The War of the Sexes: How Conflict and Cooperation Have Shaped Men and Women from Prehistory to the Present*. Princeton: Princeton University Press.

Shakespeare, William. 2005. *The Complete Works.* Ed. Stanley Wells and Gary Taylor. 2d ed. Oxford: Clarendon Press.

Sidanius, Jim, and Felicia Pratto. 1999. *Social Dominance: An Intergroup Theory of Social Hierarchy and Oppression.* Cambridge: Cambridge University Press.

Sidney, Sir Philip. 1989. *Sir Philip Sidney: A Critical Edition of the Major Works.* Ed. Katherine Duncan-Jones. Oxford: Oxford University Press.

Simonton, Dean Keith. 1999. *Origins of Genius: Darwinian Perspectives on Creativity.* New York: Oxford University Press.

Singh, Jyotsna G. 2007. " 'Th' expense of spirit in a waste of shame': Mapping the 'Emotional Regime' of Shakespeare's Sonnets." In Schoenfeldt, 277–289.

Solomon, Sheldon, Jeff Greenberg, and Tom Pyszczynski. 1998. "Tales from the Crypt: On the Role of Death in Life." *Zygon* 33(1): 9–43.

———. 2004. "The Cultural Animal: Twenty Years of Terror Management Theory and Research." In *Handbook of Experimental Existential Psychology,* ed. J. Greenberg, S. L. Koole, and T. Pyszczynski. New York: Guilford, 13–34.

Solomon, Sheldon, J. Greenberg, J. Schimel, J. Arndt, and T. Pyszczynski. 2004. "Human Awareness of Mortality and the Evolution of Culture." In *The Psychological Foundations of Culture,* ed. M. Schaller and C. Crandall. New York: Erlbaum, 15–40.

Spenser, Edward. 1997. *Edward Spenser's Amoretti and Epithalamion: A Critical Edition.* Ed. Kenneth Larsen. Tempe, Ariz.: Medieval and Renaissance Texts and Studies.

Sperber, Dan, ed. 2000. *Metarepresentations: A Multidisciplinary Perspective.* Oxford: Oxford University Press.

Sperber, Dan, and Deirdre Wilson. 1988. *Relevance: Communication and Cognition.* Oxford: Blackwell.

Spiller, Michael R. G. 1997. *The Sonnet Sequence: A Study of Its Strategies.* New York: Twayne.

Strier, Richard. 2007. "The Refusal to Be Judged in Petrarch and Shakespeare." In Schoenfeldt, 73–89.

Swirski, Peter. 2010. *Literature, Analytically Speaking: Explorations in the Theory of Interpretation, Analytic Aesthetics, and Evolution.* Austin: University of Texas Press.

Taylor, Gary. 1989. *Reinventing Shakespeare: A Cultural History, from the Restoration to the Present.* New York: Weidenfeld and Nicolson.

Tomasello, Michael. 1995. "Joint Attention as Social Cognition." In *Joint Attention: Its Origins and Role in Development,* ed. C. Moore and P. Dunham. Hillsdale, N.J.: Lawrence Erlbaum, 103–130.

———. 2008. *The Origins of Human Communication.* Cambridge, Mass.: MIT Press.

Tomasello, Michael, Melinda Carpenter, Josep Call, Tanya Behne, and Henrike Moll. 2005. "Understanding and Sharing Intentions: The Origins of Cultural Cognition." *Behavioral and Brain Sciences* 28: 675–735.

Tooby, John, and Leda Cosmides. 1996. "Friendship and the Banker's Paradox: Other Pathways to the Evolution of Adaptations for Altruism." *Proceedings of the British Academy* 88: 119–143.

———. 2001. "Does Beauty Build Adapted Minds? Towards an Evolutionary Theory of Aesthetics, Function, and the Arts." *SubStance* 20(12): 6–27.

Traversi, Derek A. 1938/1968. *An Approach to Shakespeare.* 3d ed. London: Hollis and Carter.

Trevarthen, Colwyn. 1979. "Communication and Cooperation in Early Infancy: A Description of Primary Intersubjectivity." In *Before Speech: The Beginnings of Human Communication,* ed. M. Bullowa. Cambridge: Cambridge University Press, 321–347.

Trevor, Douglas. 2007. "Shakespeare's Love Objects." In Schoenfeldt, 225–241.

Trivers, Robert. 1972. "Parental Investment and Sexual Selection." In *Sexual Selection and the Descent of Man: 1871–1971,* ed. B. Campbell. Chicago: Aldine, 163–179.

Tsur, Reuven. 1998. *Poetic Rhythm: Structure and Performance—An Empirical Study in Cognitive Poetics.* Bern: Peter Lang.

Turner, Frederick, and Ernst Pöppel. 1988. "Metered Poetry, the Brain, and Time." In *Beauty and the Brain: Biological Aspects of Aesthetics,* ed. I. Rentschler, B. Hertzberger, and D. Epstein. Basel: Birkhäuser, 71–90.

Vanderbeke, Dirk. 2010. "Rhymes without Reason? Or: The Improbable Evolution of Poetry." *Politics and Culture* 1, http://www.politicsandculture.org/2010/04/29/rhymes-withoutreason-or-the-improbable-evolution-of-poetry/.

Vendler, Helen. 1994. "Shakespeare's Sonnets: Reading for Difference." *Bulletin of the American Academy of Arts and Sciences* 47: 33–50.

——, ed. 1997/1999. *The Art of Shakespeare's Sonnets.* Cambridge, Mass.: Belknap Press of Harvard University Press

Verhagen, Arie. 2007. "Construal and Perspectivization." In *The Oxford Handbook of Cognitive Linguistics,* ed. Dirk Geeraerts and Hubert Cuckyens. Oxford: Oxford University Press, 48–81.

Vermeule, Blakey. 2010. *Why Do We Care about Literary Characters?* Baltimore: Johns Hopkins University Press.

Vickers, Brian. 2007. *Shakespeare, "A Lover's Complaint" and John Davies of Hereford.* Cambridge: Cambridge University Press.

Wells, Stanley. 2010. *Shakespeare, Sex, and Love.* Oxford: Oxford University Press.

West, David, ed. 2007. *Shakespeare's Sonnets with a New Commentary.* London: Duckworth Overlook.

Wilbur, Richard. 1976. *Responses: Prose Pieces: 1953–1976.* New York: Harcourt Brace Jovanovich.

Williams, William Carlos. 1986. *The Collected Poems of William Carlos Williams.* Vol. 1. Ed. A. Walton Litz and Christopher McGowan. Manchester: Carcanet.

Wilson, David Sloan. 2002. *Darwin's Cathedral: Evolution, Religion, and the Nature of Society.* Chicago: University of Chicago Press.

——. 2005. "Evolutionary Social Constructivism." In Gottschall and Wilson, 20–37.

——. 2007a. *Evolution for Everyone: How Darwin's Theory Can Change the Way We Think about Our Lives.* New York: Delacorte.

——. 2007b. Foreword. In Barbara Oakley, *Evil Genes: Why Rome Fell, Hitler Rose, Enron Failed, and My Sister Stole My Mother's Boyfriend.* Amherst, N.Y.: Prometheus Books.

Wilson, David Sloan, and E. O. Wilson. 2007. "Rethinking the Theoretical Foundations of Sociobiology." *Quarterly Review of Biology* 82: 327–348.

Wilson, E. O. 1975/2000. *Sociobiology: The New Synthesis.* 25th Anniversary ed. Cambridge, Mass.: Belknap Press of Harvard University Press.

Winkelman, Michael A. 2009. "Sighs and Tears: Biological Signals and John Donne's 'Whining Poetry.'" *Philosophy and Literature* 33: 329–344.

Wordsworth, William. 1984. *William Wordsworth.* Ed. Stephen Gill. Oxford: Oxford University Press.

———. 2004. *Sonnet Series and Itinerary Poems, 1820–1845.* Ed. Geoffrey Jackson. Ithaca: Cornell University Press.

Wroth, Lady Mary. 1996/2010. *Lady Mary Wroth: Poems: A Modernized Edition.* Ed. R. E. Pritchard. Edinburgh: Edinburgh University Press.

Zahavi, Amotz, and Avishag Zahavi. 1997. *The Handicap Principle: A Missing Piece of Darwin's Puzzle.* Oxford: Oxford University Press.

Zunshine, Lisa, ed. 2010. *Introduction to Cognitive Cultural Studies.* Baltimore: Johns Hopkins University Press.

Index